HAPPIER THAN A

BILLIONAIRE

NADINE HAYS PISANI

DEDICATION

To Rob. It's funnier with you by my side.

CONTENTS

Part III

ACKNOWLEDGEMENTS

Many thanks to my wonderful family, especially to my mother and father who took me to the Metropolitan Museum of Art when I was a child and showed me this world is a big place worthy of exploring. I must recognize my sister, Stacey, who said she did not want to be in the acknowledgements because no one ever reads them. But it's important to thank her for her tireless hours of reading my scribble and making editorial suggestions. Also, without her locking me in a suitcase when I was five, I would never have acquired the travel bug so soon in life.

And to my beautiful nieces: Diana, Veronica, and Anastasia. I see your eyes in every child I pass.

Part I

Dear Job... We Need To Talk

Did this just happen? My patient farted on me... literally. This one is particularly brutal and my eyes burn as if sprayed with extra-strength bear mace. It's a whopper. I nonchalantly open the door so that my secretary can share in my misery. She came in late today, and there is no better way to punish her then to subject her to a little chemical warfare. There is no time to escape; she folds quicker than an advancing Italian army.

Of course, my patient pretends it wasn't him; they never take responsibility. I'm backfired on at least half a dozen times a day, and not once does anyone apologize or say excuse me. They all stare straight ahead and continue complaining about their lousy spouse or deadbeat kid. It makes me want to drink on the job—not beer or wine, but strictly the top shelf hard stuff. I need maximum inebriation to handle days like this.

God, I hate my job. In fact, I hate it so much that if you love your job I might just hate you, too. This has prevented me from enjoying anyone's happiness lately. I'm at my worst when I collapse on the couch after work and turn on Rachael Ray. She looks so damn happy I want to punch her in the face. What kind of person wants to assault the lovely Rachael Ray?

I shouldn't use the word hate. A word that strong should be reserved for the emotion felt toward dictators, menstrual cramps, and those health conscious people who substitute oil in brownies with applesauce. It's not like I have the worst job. I am a chiropractor, but being one means opening a Pandora's Box at a party, never knowing if someone likes what you do or is prepared to berate you for not being a *real* doctor. I love the way they say the word *real*. Like I'm trying to pass off that I'm the Easter Bunny. Instead, I lie and tell them I'm a government administrator. A job so incredibly nondescript that their eyes instantly glaze over as if they just popped 10mg of Ambien.

Knowing that I chose the wrong career makes me feel like I have a *Keep On Trucking* tattoo on my face. It's permanent, and no matter how many trips I take to the laser clinic, it can't be removed. In order to get through my day knowing I'll spend the rest of my life in this office, I've taken up reading TripAdvisor.com reviews during my lunch break. Not the gleaming five star winners, but those that are so wonderfully negative. I actually feel better when I read about other people's crappy vacations.

My preferred genre is the bad reviews for luxury hotels, the Ritz-Carlton and Four Seasons being two of my favorites. The idea of someone spending fifteen hundred dollars a night on a room with a broken air conditioner overlooking a bus depot is enchanting. It's almost as good as Googling old boyfriends and discovering they're unemployed and bald.

Today, a man from London wrote a scathing review of a room where he found a booger on the bedpost. An atrocity so disturbing his wife collapsed to the floor in a fit of hysterics. I find this not at all surprising. The bourgeois are especially unrealistic, and most of their reviews end with a woman collapsing into a deranged mess of unconsciousness. I can understand a sticky snot would be disturbing, but falling into pupil- dilating shock? The horrible nightmare continued when the man found the tiles in the bathroom were made of porcelain instead of marble (an offense easy to discover since he was already on his hands and knees giving mouth-to-mouth to his convulsing wife on the floor). My sister once stayed at a hotel and reclined into an undetermined wet spot on her bed. She didn't lose consciousness once, and we're all but certain the suspicious wet spot was something infinitely worse than a booger on a bedpost.

In addition to reading TripAdvisor reviews, I am experimenting with another method to cheer myself up: wearing bright blue scrubs to work. Mostly because they feel like pajamas, and I have a theory it will improve my sappy temperament. The ample hip room alone is graciously accommodating to the additional fifteen pounds of saddlebags I gained since starting work. But after recognizing my body is morphing into the shape of a Bartlett pear, I bury my face in a pillow and realize I am not only depressed but quickly becoming fat *and* depressed.

This is a combination so attractive I celebrate by ordering useless items off QVC. Tonight I decide on a fake fur coat.

I love calling and chatting it up with the operators, talking as if we are close girlfriends hanging out on my dorm room bed reading the astrology section of Cosmo magazine. After giving my name (no need to give payment method—they already have my credit card on file), I prolong the exchange by asking insanely stupid questions like, "Is the faux white coat fire retardant?" I reach down into my Doritos bag as she explains my coat will not ignite spontaneously and suggests I order online next time. I don't tell her that my orange Dorito fingers will stain my keyboard, and after a dose of late night television shopping, I can't leave any trace of evidence behind. So I pretend I don't own a computer. I am now lying to my imaginary QVC girlfriend.

This personality shift is due to the fact that I made a horrible mistake with the direction of my life. It's apparent I will never cruise the Mediterranean on a private yacht. Not that it was the barometer for a happy life, but in my twenties that dream actually seemed plausible: that somehow, George Clooney would find my personality irresistible and ask me to meet him in Portofino for finger sandwiches. Sadly, it's not going to happen. Instead, I'm looking at thirty years to life at being a participating provider at most health insurance companies. What a buzzkill.

Now I am deciding to break up with my job. I wrestle with this speech in my mind as if I am preparing to dump a future ex-boyfriend. "It's not you; it's me. Although we gave it our best shot, I just don't think we are right for each other. Plus, I am not attracted to you anymore. You've gotten sloppy and let yourself go. But before I leave, can I have my Neil Diamond CD back?"

I plan to share all of this with my husband, but he is projectile vomiting in the bathroom at the moment. He hates his job, too.

Under The Central American Sun

My husband, Rob, is the easiest going guy you'll ever meet. I once smacked a meatball sandwich out of his hand while we were bickering, scattering the tomato sauce across the floor like a Jackson Pollock painting. "Hey, I was eating that," was all he could say before returning to the kitchen. It's impossible to argue with a man who never wants to argue; who just wants to make himself another meatball sandwich instead of continuing a fight.

Although my husband is a born optimist and has the patience of a saint, he, too, is getting tired of being a chiropractor. But instead of becoming a professional complainer like me, he has embarked on a bizarre campaign of puking everywhere we go. I urge him to see a doctor, but he is hesitant, blaming the symptoms on all the stress at work.

It's not unlike him to avoid doctors. He once sliced open his upper thigh with a large box cutter and never made one complaint. Instead of getting stitches, he wrapped duct tape around his leg and secured it under his buttock to close the laceration. He walked around like that for a week, even as the duct tape ripped off most of his pubic hair. During this same period, I stepped on my hairdryer plug and collapsed in a theatrical performance that could have landed me the role as Scarlett O'Hara. My husband, in a typical act of chivalry, picked me up off the floor and carried me to the bed. Although bending over ripped out the remaining hair along his testicle, the man still didn't complain. Unless Rob is dying, he's not going to see a doctor.

In addition to his regurgitating problem, Rob has been notably quiet lately. He doesn't talk much and sits in front of his two hundred and sixty-five gallon fish tank for hours after work. As his job becomes more demanding, so do the contents of the tank. What was once a cute little goldfish community has now transformed into the Great Barrier Reef. This is where I find him after returning home from a grueling ten-hour day in the office.

"Did you know that a clown fish lives inside an anemone his entire life?" He gestures to a small fish in the corner of the aquarium. "That fish will never know what's on the other side of the tank. Don't you think human beings are like that too? We spend most of our lives in an office and then retire in the same city we've been living in the past thirty years. Rarely does anyone bother to swim to the other side of the tank."

I look down and see a pile of papers on the floor. I find full pages dedicated to financial calculations, algorithms, and pie charts where Rob has punched in every aspect of our life. There is an Excel graph listing everything we own and the corresponding fair market price. The only things not on the list are the pets and me. It's a good thing; I wouldn't want to know what the going rate is for an irritable thirty-seven year old woman.

Rob confides he wants to quit his job. "It's killing me. I feel like vomiting every day. I wake up each morning with a pit in my stomach fearing I will spend the rest of my life in that office." This is not a surprise; we are both burnt out from our careers. I just choose to be bitchy while he prefers upchucking in the Olive Garden parking lot.

"I think about it, too," I tell him. "I actually dream of walking out of there and never going back. But how can we possibly do it? We're too young to retire. Who thinks of retiring in their mid-thirties?" Even though he is reading my mind, it all seems hopeless.

It's not like we all didn't dream of doing something different with our lives. After establishing a career, it doesn't make sense to change, even if you are miserable. Now that my future seems cemented in one place, I often wonder how my life could have looked if I decided to go down a different road, if I had taken more chances.

My sister once confided that she used to dream her life would include Broadway shows and fancy dinners at the trendiest restaurants. She truly believed her life would play out like the society section of *Town & Country Magazine*. The reality is she changes diapers and has poison control on speed dial. I thought the latter was a tad overprotective until I discovered my two-year-old niece recently climbed onto the kitchen counter and guzzled a half bottle of wine. Maybe I should be asking her these pressing questions since she, too, feels the urge to drink in the middle of the day.

There was no need to go any further with the conversation. My sister will never be that woman jetting off to a Broadway show. She is a mom in suburbia living a comfortable life with her loving family. Nevertheless, I know she still longs to be her doppelganger: living it up in the city, eating ridiculously expensive dinners, and enjoying overpriced Broadway shows.

I don't give much thought to Rob's early retirement proposal, but he insists he's thought it through and has come up with a master plan. "If we do quit our jobs, we can't live anywhere in the United States. The federal, state, property, and school taxes combined make it unaffordable. But we could move to another country. You're always reading books like *Under the Tuscan Sun* or *A Year in Provence*. Look what those people did."

"You think we can afford someplace like that? Like France or Tuscany?" I eagerly reply.

"Well no. I didn't say that. We would have to settle on... how can I say this... elegantly rural." As we continue this conversation, I start to get excited when he lists the places he researched. He quickly rambles off Tahiti, the Bahamas, and St Thomas.

"Wow, those places sound great. Are they possible options?"

"No," he says. "They are too expensive. Even if we try to work as chiropractors, we could never make it there. Instead, I found a solution that will include quitting our jobs and living in a warmer climate." He leans in, takes a long pause, and unveils his crafty plan, "I've been thinking about Central America."

Dear George Clooney,
No need to wait for me in Portofino since I will be busy admitting my husband to an inpatient mental facility.

Warmest Regards,
Nadine

Do You Know The Way To San Jose?

My mind goes through a Central American slide show filled with images of poverty, dysentery, and those fastidious Sandinistas who gave Ollie North such a headache in the 1980s. I never considered moving anywhere south of California, but I have to admit: despite all my fears, quitting and starting a new life does sound tempting. Moreover, my faux fur coat has arrived; the sleeves are a foot longer than my arms, and the lining resembles Huggy Bear's jacket from Starsky and Hutch. I look like a five-foot version of a pimped out abominable snowman. Now might be the perfect time to quit my obsession with QVC and look for enjoyment that doesn't involve an item number with a convenient four-easy-payment plan. For the first time in a very long time, the thought of throwing in the towel and never walking into that office gives me a euphoric high that I don't want to end.

It turns out Rob already investigated and eliminated many possible countries. Whether for immigration problems, infrastructure, or the higher statistical risk of having our bludgeoned bodies thrown into a ditch, we will not be living in Guatemala, Honduras, Mexico, or Nicaragua. "El Salvador is up and coming," he says with confidence, as if we are discussing the redevelopment project in Coney Island. "But their history with a recent bloody civil war makes them an unstable option." It's sweet; after all these years, my husband still shields me from unsavory political uprisings. He considered Belize for its awesome circular reef called the Blue Hole. However, inadequate health care and high crime rates made him scrap that idea and look farther south. Costa Rica seemed to have it all.

I repeat the name Costa Rica over and over again in my head. Maybe they are different from their tumultuous neighbors. I can already hear Ricardo Montalban and his sassy sidekick Tattoo welcoming me to the island before whisking me off on an awe-inspiring adventure. It sounds dreamlike, even though I know absolutely nothing about the country. My curiosity soon changes into heart palpitating fear. Who, with only one conversation with her husband, is going to pick up everything and move to a country where she doesn't know the language, or where it is on a map? I shouldn't even be contemplating this. One half of me considers my husband's plan while the other half wants to move all of our assets out of his name and hire Gloria Allred to hold a press conference. But, I've missed so many opportunities to travel; maybe he's not so crazy and I need to roll the dice on this one.

I have a history of passing up great adventures. Instead of backpacking across Europe with my friends, I chose to save my money for graduate school. In lieu of going on spring break, I had an artist paint a palm tree landscape across my dorm room wall. It's sad that I stared at a mural of palm trees instead of actually going somewhere to see them in person. It appears I have been holding onto all of these pictures in my mind a little too long. It's time to change all that.

In the end, I would rather make a colossal mistake instead of not taking the chance. My biggest fear is that I will look back at the decision and horribly regret that I didn't move. Deciding to embark on this adventure will definitely make up for all those times I decided to take the more responsible route. Before I commit whole-heartedly, I have to do a little investigating on my own about Costa Rica. First and most importantly… where is it?

Unbeknownst to me and many other people I talk to, Costa Rica is not an island. It has the Caribbean Sea to the east and the Pacific Ocean to the west. Its northern border is Nicaragua, where the infamous Contra War occurred against the opposing Sandinista faction.

Unlike Nicaragua, Costa Rica has a relatively peaceful existence with a democratic government. It has remained a calm oasis despite the unrest in other Central American countries. Costa Rica doesn't even have a military; it was abolished in 1949. The capital, San Jose, has a sophisticated socialized health care system. In fact, Costa Rica's health care system ranks higher than that of the United States. Everyone has access to a doctor, and the government pays for it all. Chief exports are bananas, pineapples, and coffee. However, its major sources of income are tourism and medical treatments, bringing more money into the country than all three exports combined. Who wouldn't want to travel to see all those cute monkeys and sloths while recovering from a reasonably priced facelift? Snap open the Botox and sign me up.

Moving to Costa Rica will also require me to prioritize my life. If I plan to move twenty-two hundred miles away, I will need to get rid of a lot of my possessions and change the way I live. It could be the best thing to happen to me, but it is a complete paradigm shift from how I was raised.

I come from a long line of hard working relatives. Some took a boat over the Atlantic to find a better life, while others were orphaned at a young age and hopped rail cars across the country to find work. My father, for example, became deaf in his thirties and still took a bus to New York City every day to work. His father had a stroke at a young age and continued his job in a factory with only one functioning arm. As a result, having a good time never seemed to be high on my parents' list of priorities. You can find proof of this by browsing through photos of my childhood. In every one of them, I have an expression similar to that found at a Russian bread line after WWII; even then, my Nana would have told me to stop looking like I was enjoying myself.

If you whine to my family about your job, you will get the amount of sympathy that you surely deserve—absolutely none. Life is tough, unfair, and you have to work much harder than the person next to you if you want to succeed.

Rob, on the other hand, is a fun loving guy. His Italian family, especially his uncles, love to play cards and have a good time. Their weddings are an explosion in laughter, dancing, and the occasional fisticuffs. I once saw his uncle knock a guy out at a wedding, drag him by his heels to the street, and then go back inside to continue the chicken dance. In addition, Rob's grandfather did not want him to work his whole life. He wanted his grandson to recognize that time goes by in a flash, replacing a once agile body with aching joints and arthritic fingers. This advice must have stuck because Rob doesn't want to wait any longer. We have been unhappy for too long, and he feels it is the perfect time to turn it all around.

I'm anxious to read further and learn more about my possible new home. I punch Costa Rica into a search engine on my laptop, and a lengthy list of diseases pop up on my screen, some so weird and disturbing I would rather break bread with the Sandinistas.

Disease... It's What's For Dinner

There must be nothing as unimaginably gruesome as finding larvae buried under your skin. I'm confident that if I remain in Pennsylvania this will probably never happen to me. Although I run the risk of my entire town being engulfed in a nuclear winter by the nearby Three Mile Island plant, oddly this doesn't bother me as much as the thought of eggs hatching and worming their way around my epidermis. Surely, the most nauseating thing that can happen to a person.

Apparently, the botfly is responsible for such an achievement. This little go-getter implants its larvae under the scalp, and the host never feels anything until the maggots start wiggling their slimy bodies. It is not an easy thing to diagnose. At first, the doctor will think you have an infection. No one is likely to believe that you feel something squirming under your skin—in fact, they will adamantly conclude you have lost your mind. And just as your family is about to commit you to Bellevue, out pops a ghastly looking head before jutting back inside its warm and cozy hole. This is when you can have your I-told-you-so moment and show Dr. Schmutzo the cunning critter who has taken refuge in your noggin. You can try to coax it out with meat, "Come on out, mommy has a treat for you," or if bacon isn't handy, try smearing the hole with Vaseline, and the sucker will come up for air. At that point, you can grab it at the base with a pair of tweezers and yank it out. It all sounds like a bad Sci-Fi movie starring Stephen Baldwin and Lorenzo Lamos.

I repeat some of these charming findings to Rob, who dismisses them with a quick, "What are the odds?" He is always fast to disregard something that doesn't neatly fit into his modus operandi. Once, in Jamaica, he went head first down a crude slide built into a cliff. When I realized no one else was doing this, I yelled out that he could hurt himself. Rob responded with a tapering "What are the odds?" before landing in the water and resurfacing with a dislocated shoulder. The odds turned out that I got stuck schlepping our luggage around for the rest of the vacation. All the worse because he insisted we bring one Tyrannosaurus Rex sized suitcase that he would, of course, carry during the trip. Rob might have good intentions, but he also has a history of disregarding the advice of his awesomely brilliant wife. And a botfly to him is just a small inconvenience when compared to the bigger picture of living in utopia. A utopia that clearly includes bugs that feast on your head.

After reading about the botfly, I continue to the next link: one dedicated specifically to diarrhea and all the ways to acquire it. Diarrhea is the Mac Daddy of all maladies, an exploding, cascading river of unpleasantness that afflicts hikers who explore the rainforest as well as the average traveler who decides to plop an unassuming ice cube in their Diet Coke. It is the biggest killer and can be caused by a number of things: E. coli and other bacteria, viruses, parasites, and protozoa. Basically, what will most likely kill you is not the actual disease but the resulting diarrhea that follows. I am a petite woman, and a bad bout of diarrhea can have me dangerously dehydrated in a couple days. I know this first hand from an unfortunate incident following a Taco Bell

Burrito Supreme. Although moving to a place with eternal sunshine sounds pleasant, so does keeping my large intestines from bursting.

Another bug that can cause distress is the sand fly, with its vector borne disease Leishmaniasis. The parasites can spread from the skin to the inside of the nose and other mucus membranes, causing extensive ulcerative damage. This is interesting since it originates from something as ordinary as a sand fly. There have even been recorded cases of this type of fly in Florida and other states. It starts out as an ordinary bug bite and can progress into something as sinister as skin sores and organ damage. This changes the image I have of myself sitting at the beach, one moment sipping my piña colada, the other fanatically swatting kidney killing flies away from me with my rolled up National Enquirer. And from the photos I have seen, these flies seem to like the most unfortunate of places such as eyelids and lips. Good thing plastic surgery is cheap in Costa Rica.

The list goes on and on: warnings about roundworms and malaria, diseases that can cause blindness and hemodynamic collapse. (I have no idea what that is, but it sounds infinitely worse than collapsing after stepping on a hair dryer plug.) A whole chapter is dedicated to precautions associated with exploring abandoned mines and bat caves. This is an actual highlighted warning: "If you are about to frolic through a bat cave it is best to avoid rubbing bat excrement on your hands and arms." Really? Isn't that already implied? How about not frolicking in a bat cave in the first place?

I repeat my research findings to Rob, but he is too busy calling airlines. He has already made up his mind. Regardless of the things I have uncovered, he is going to Costa Rica to see for himself. Now is about the time I could reconsider the whole thing. I could make a firm and declaratory statement to my husband—an executive decision as I like to call it—that under the present circumstances and short incubation periods of the above diseases, this is not a place I want to live. But even with the threat of blindness, a wormy scalp, and deadly diarrhea, it's sad to say that it all sounds much better than another day in the office. I hate my job so much that I am prepared, if necessary, to coax a worm out of my head with baloney.

All this would make for interesting conversation and would stop people from razzing me about being a chiropractor. A stint in the rainforest will definitely raise my level of coolness and layer my presently boring personality. Instead of an office lackey, I could be an adventurer who just made the cover of *Outside Magazine*. At the next party, I'll compete with that poncho-wearing guy who tells stories about his first expedition to Mt. Everest: "It was at base camp that my Sherpa's yak suddenly fell ill. Thankfully, the mountain did not claim my frostbitten big toe." I don't care how cold it gets in Kathmandu, prodding a maggot out of your scalp with a pastrami sandwich is freakishly more fabulous.

And, 'more fabulous' is what I am going for. Instead of my trials and tribulations with my faulty all-in-one fax machine, I can tell a tale that takes place outside the office under the rainforest canopy. I am one bout of dysentery away from weaving my own harrowing story. Wanderlust is waiting for me. I just need to be brave enough to take the next step, and since Rob just booked two tickets to Costa Rica for next week, I guess the decision is already made.

"Fortunately, I was wearing my Italian cap toe oxfords. Sophisticated yet different; nothing to make a huge fuss about. Rich dark brown calfskin leather. Matching leather vent. Men's whole and half sizes 7 through 13. Price: $135.00."
                                                    -J. Peterman (Seinfeld)

I am listening to a group of guys planning to surf at Witch's Rock. They talk a language I can hardly understand: words like epic, cut back, and nose dive. Their energy is contagious while they share animated tales of other surfing trips in Australia and South Africa. I first noticed them in line at the ticket counter. Their hair is bleached from the sun, and even the darkest of the group has blond highlights in his black curly locks. Each casually carries a surfboard under an arm with a backpack slung over one shoulder. Do all surfers travel with their surfboards instead of renting one at the destination? You must really love to surf if you are willing to lug a board across the world. I'm feeling like a teenager again, and these are the cool kids I want to befriend. I now want to learn how to surf.

I notice small tribes of people with unfamiliar gear chatting about their adrenaline-packed adventures. Nobody on this flight is going to Costa Rica to lie on the beach. If you were, I fear it would be like saying you went to the Louvre and didn't bother to see the Mona Lisa. I break the spine opening our *Lonely Planet Travel Guide* and name all the exciting things we can do outside of frying my ghostly white skin with equator-strength sunshine. I read the list out loud so other passengers know that I am an adrenaline-packed badass as well.

"Wow, we can rappel down waterfalls; doesn't that sound great?" I say to Rob.

"Are you kidding? The water will be freezing, and a squirrel carcass can smack you in the head," he says as he points out a cat toilet training system in *Sky Mall* magazine. His reply is not what I expected, but I continue in my loud voice as I dramatically list the crazy activities we can do. I make sure the cool surfer kids can hear me as I confirm the class four white rapids that, of course, I will be completing on my trip.

However, we will not be doing any death-defying stunts, no rappelling or zip lines. There will not be enough time. If we want to move there, it's important that we investigate prices of real estate. The only hiking we decided on was in the national parks to check out the howler monkeys and sloths. With that in mind, I needed to buy a couple pairs of hiking pants to protect me from all the little critters that are likely to bite my ankles while in the rainforest.

A couple days before our flight, I visited an outdoor sporting store, a place where kayaks hang from ceilings and dazzling para-sailing displays hog the middle of the floor. It's fair to say it was all very intimidating, especially after watching a saleswoman wearing a Live Strong bracelet chat with another globe trekker about BASE jumping off a cliff in Chile. I should have stuck with Lady Foot Locker.

I maneuvered past the towering Columbia Anti-Trail Grit shoe display and walked straight to the clothing section. It was much more complicated than the average lumbering traveler could ever imagine. It's not simply about buying pants, something I presumed I was more than capable of doing.

Not to boast, but I've been picking out my clothes since the first day my mother pulled into the Sears parking lot with our big red Chevy Impala, a car so fuel inefficient it was single-handedly responsible for the infamous gas crunch of the 1970's, resulting with the Shah of Iran fleeing his homeland. After ten minutes of my mother navigating the behemoth into a parking space, my sister and I would rip our sweaty thighs off the vinyl seats and dash into the children's Garanimals department.

With the clothes organized by color and animal, I found immediate success by matching my polyester purple hippo pants to the purple hippo top. "Easy to pair, fun to wear" was my motto. We would end the victorious day of shopping by eating in the store's cafeteria, my sister and I gleaming over our fashionable monochromatic purchases while eating a platter of Salisbury steak with mashed potatoes.

With a successful history of pants shopping under my belt, I thought I could grab a couple pair off the rack in the sporting goods store with just enough time to buy a few Cinnabons at the mall across the street. I quickly learned that this shopping trip wasn't just about buying pants but about ensuring my survival. I felt energy surge through my blood stream as I reached for a pair of pants made out of moisture- wicking fabric injected with mosquito retardant technology. To my right were slacks with zippers that turned into shorts and shorts with zippers that turned into secret pockets. Then I saw the holy grail of pants—a pair with a patented gusseted crotch capable of negotiating the increased degree of movement needed for extreme vacationing. All the clothes came with bright and colorful informative tags suggesting bold ways in which to experience the product:

"Our combination pants are perfect while eating a fish taco at the beach before dune buggying until dusk."

Wow, this guy has me pegged. Now I see why I need that extra roomy crotch. I made a note to put dune buggying on my list of things to do. Apparently, my pants demand this caliber of entertainment. I then walked ten feet to the hat section, only to find it had its own Linnaeus classification system: wide and short brim, wind and water repellant. There were even hats that came with built-in sunblock, which, when you think about it, seemed unnecessary since blocking the sun was the function of a hat in the first place.

I brought a few pieces of clothing and the matching mildew resistant explorer hat into the fitting room. I walked out resembling an emasculated Ernest Hemingway on an African safari. I looked like, as my father would say, a horse's ass. It's a favorite expression of his, used only to describe the worst of pretentious offenders. I heard him first mumble it under his breath when I was four years old after witnessing a man wearing tight white linen pants on the beach. He also repeated it after watching a gentleman with a preppy sweater draped backwards over his shoulder test the screw-top house wine that came free with dinner, swirl it delicately in the glass, then sip it before nodding his approval to the waiter. "What's the horse's ass going to do?" my dad said. "Spit it out and ask for another bottle of free wine?"

With my father's voice ringing in my head, it was obvious that this outfit was guilty of a venerable minefield of offenses, so unless I was planning to shoot a rhinoceros in the next half hour, I knew I should remove them. Before I did, I looked down at the price tags, and the outfit alone cost more than my airplane ticket. Was all this really necessary? Even Jane Goodall doesn't spend one hundred dollars on moisture- wicking fabric. There were vents in areas I wasn't sure I wanted vented and so many snaps I couldn't figure out what they all snapped to. I finally took off the hat and shirt and snapped both to the pants before racing out of the store.

This entire outdoor-adventure style looked to me like a couture line of military clothing not so overpowering as wearing camouflage pants, but having the same effect: standing out in the crowd. It also reminded me of those kids in high school who came to class every day in full military outfits, including regulation black lace-up boots. Back then, we just thought they were eccentric. I now realize I was one smart-ass comment away from getting blown away in homeroom.

Sitting on the plane, I can see that I really didn't need to take a loan out to buy a new wardrobe. Except for a few individuals, almost everyone is wearing T-shirts and flip-flops. And those surfers that I wanted to befriend so badly are stealing the unwashed airplane blankets and sticking them into their backpacks. One surfer tells the flight attendant they are staying at a ten dollar a night hostel and asks for an extra bag of peanuts. I guess flying around the world to surf takes a tremendous amount of sacrifice and requires a diet heavy in free salted nuts. I am not enamored by them anymore, the allure erased by the thought of sleeping on a lice- infested pillow.

Right when I'm about to sit back and enjoy the in-flight movie, a middle-aged man wearing convertible pants and anti-grit trail boots gets up to go to the bathroom. What's most spectacular about this moment is that he keeps his khaki explorer hat on in the cabin. The passenger must be under the impression there is a chance for rain in our tightly sealed fuselage. I follow him to the bathroom, where I overhear him tell another man that he is staying at the Four Seasons. I can already picture him with his moleskin journal recording his nightly observations:

My Dearest Sylvia,

I had just returned from documenting the mating ritual of the leaf cutter ant when I sadly realized my manservant had not run my bath or turned down the duvet. It pains me to be so far away.

Your Betrothed,
Bartholomew Bungholio

I wish my father were here to witness this. It would make his day to add another entry on his long established list of schmaltzy nitwits. I doze off forgetting about the people on the plane, replacing them with thoughts of what the next twenty-four hours will bring, and I hope this crazy idea of ours has legs to stand on.

The Pothole Chronicles

Our car rental agreement will not cover any damage to our tires; the roads have too many potholes. All four tires could spontaneously fly off our car and we would still be held responsible for their replacements. With no other choice, Rob signs the contract and asks for a map of Costa Rica. We have a seven hour ride ahead of us with only one hour left before the sun sets. To save money, we flew into the San Jose Airport in the middle of the country. A wiser, more expensive flight to Liberia Airport would have landed us an hour away from our intended destination, Tamarindo. This error in judgment will have us driving across the country in the dark.

I am uneasy with this plan. Now that we are here, I don't have that super inquisitive feeling I usually get when I travel. The representative hands us the map and highlights our zigzag route. It's not a straight shot, and I can already see the countless ways we can get lost. I run my finger along the map and consider the crossroads I should watch out for. "Will the signs be illuminated?" I ask. He stares at me as if I just demanded samples of the interstellar dust surrounding the Milky Way Galaxy.

"There are no signs," he says. "Costa Rica has very few road signs. Follow the road and take careful notice of the towns you drive through. Also, this is the worst rainy season on record, so be very careful. That's the best advice I can give you."

It's hard to fathom a country not dominated by signs. In America, we are obsessed by them. On our family vacation to Disney World, we drove Route 95 from New Jersey to Florida. Once reaching Virginia, we came upon signs advertising a roadside attraction called *South of the Border*. There were more than two hundred billboards showing a cute little Mexican guy named Pedro speaking culturally insensitive phrases like "Put Some Junque een Your Trunque" and "You Never Sausage a Place." At eight years old, I found these billboards hilarious, and the "Chili today, Hot Tamale" joke was enthusiastically added to my already wildly successful stand-up routine in gym class. South of the Border promised an oasis of hospitality with "easy on, easy off" gas fueling, cheap fireworks, and an amusement park with a state-of-the-art game room. High with the thought of blowing ten dollars' worth of quarters in a Space Invaders machine, it made me reconsider why the hell we were going all the way to Florida when this Mexican hot bed of activity was only another two hundred miles away. I could hardly wait for little Pedro to welcome me and my family.

At three in the morning, we saw in the distance a complex lit up like Times Square on New Year's Eve. There was Pedro, a ninety-foot, smiling, mustachioed icon dominating the horizon. Only a few hundred feet off the highway, I could see other wary travelers driving through Pedro's gigantic legs into the fantasyland of Mexican delights. My father, barely glancing at the hypnotic glowing sombrero tower, drove past the exit and continued down the darkened highway in eerie silence. Astonished, my sister and I flattened our faces against the back window and screamed like two children just abducted by a swirly hillbilly.

"I'm not stopping!" my father yelled. "The gas is two cents higher than at Texaco. Anyway, it's a tourist trap, so shut up and play your Mad Libs." And because of my father's frugal financial obligations (and the belief that Mad Libs could keep two kids entertained for a twenty-six hour car ride), we did not stop at South of the Border in 1978, and a bit of my childhood will always be lingering at the lost possibilities that existed under Pedro's pelvis.

Just as the man at the Hertz rental agency said, there are few signs to direct us toward Tamarindo. And just as he said about the rainy season, we can hardly see through the windshield. Our wipers are going full blast, but still the rain ruthlessly blinds us. There are times we are unsure if we are even traveling in the right direction. It is the first time I've ever watched a compass on the dashboard and used it for navigational purposes.

Occasionally, we come across bent, rusted signs that identify the towns we are passing. There are no street lamps, and the roads approach as endless dark tunnels. Added to the fear of getting lost and/or driving off the road, a mudslide tumbles onto the asphalt and engulfs the car in front of us. Traffic stops, and people help the man get out of his car. They all smoke cigarettes and talk under an umbrella like this is a normal occurrence on your way home from work. Soon, the men start to dig out the car, and an hour and a half later, he drives away. I wonder if he will even mention the incident to his wife.

Before we left Pennsylvania, my husband read articles about this highway. Apparently, bandits have been known to roll large boulders into the road to stop your car. They then run out, surround your car, and rob you. Although this sounds a little Wile E Coyote-ish, my husband takes it seriously and holds a tire iron in his right hand the entire car ride. I can only imagine what someone would do if they searched for crime statistics in the United States. In Tahiti, I met a Japanese lady who, in limited English, asked where I was from. When I said the US, she mimicked a gun with her fingers and hollered, "Columbine! Bang, bang, bang!" It was an interesting insight into what other nationalities think about my own country. She then turned to my husband and said he looked like Rocky. Not to disappoint his adoring Asian fan, Rob yelled, "Adrian!" and she childishly clapped her hands as if she just witnessed Sylvester Stallone himself. Years later, I still have my husband doing Rocky imitations because of some kooky Japanese lady I met on my honeymoon.

I check off each town as we pass and eventually come to The Costa Rica - Taiwan Friendship Bridge. The bridge was a gift by the Taiwanese government and cost twenty-six million dollars, but since Costa Rica has cut off relations with Taiwan to favor the Chinese, it is now known as Back Stab Bridge. The bright floodlights shine across the Tempisque River, where I can see fishermen casting their lines in the dark. This is our halfway point, and I feel reassured that we made it this far.

For the rest of the drive we do not come across any roadside attractions. There are no billboards directing us to gas stations or to restaurants promising clean bathrooms. Occasionally, we pass small souvenir stores with hammocks strung across the trees in the front. The roads are pitted with potholes, and every half hour or so we pass a car with a flat tire. My head is becoming thick with the stress of making sure we are not lost. This stress soon transforms into a full-blown migraine, and I am wishing we never came on this trip. I look out at the houses and notice they all have bars on the windows and doors. It's all painfully creepy to me.

It is two o'clock in the morning when we reach Tamarindo. We find the hotel and stumble into a lobby with one hanging fluorescent light bulb. It feels less like a tropical vacation and more like a Bangkok massage parlor. The man behind the glass hands us our key and sits back down in front of a black and white television. We walk around the outdoor pool and see a dozen surfers talking about the waves they will ride in a few hours. I think I see the same surfers from the plane. We find our cramped room: three twin beds squeezed together, blocking the entrance to the bathroom. I suppose surfers don't require much privacy or the need to get up in the middle of the night to pee. I put my head on the pillow while Rob finds me some Excedrin. This adventure isn't going as planned, and I am afraid that this rotten feeling I have won't pass. But the light of day always has a way of changing things.

Suicide Showers and Good Coffee

"Wake up, you have to come out and see this," Rob whispers before leaving the room. I open my eyes to what looks like Marcia Brady's bedroom. The bedspreads are imprinted with groovy flowers and equally un-groovy yellow stains. The misfortune continues with the curtains matching the blankets. Much of this I didn't notice last night because of my headache, but after the Excedrin and a good night's sleep, I feel much better. The two other beds block the bathroom, so I crawl across and throw my feet onto the floor. The bathroom continues with the retro color scheme: yellow tiles, yellow toilet, and yellow towels.

I open the shower curtain and see a big metal device on the end of the showerhead. Two exposed electrical wires stick out and connect to a cracked receptacle in the wall. In both English and Spanish, it reads: Danger: Do Not Touch. And just in case you might be an Inuit from Alaska who can't speak either language, there is a picture of a lightning bolt electrocuting a stick figure. The color of the lightning bolt, you guessed it, is flower power yellow.

This is my first encounter with a suicide shower, an appliance that acts as a shower head and contains an electrical coil to heat the water. The idea of electrical wires and water together make me cringe. I know the bathroom is the most dangerous room in the house, but who knew I could flirt with death just by washing my hair. I now understand why the entire room is yellow. You'll never notice the first spark.

This device could match the engineering mishaps of that devilish 1971 Ford Pinto, a stylish but affordable troublemaker that was designed in a more innocent time without car safety standards. It saddens me that the stricter automobile codes of today make it impossible for my nieces to ride in a car without seat belts. Unlike their mother and aunt, they will never experience the fanciful airborne sensation of being propelled face first into the front seat when their dad slams on the brakes.

Ford definitely took advantage of these subpar codes by marketing the Pinto with a short rear end and a gas tank situated behind the rear axle instead of above it. Although this plan saved trunk space, when struck from behind, the inadequate bumper could not prevent the gas tank from thrusting into a number of nasty sharp bolts. The tank would split open, car doors would jam, and a fiery explosion would ensue. Nonetheless, the price was right for under two thousand dollars, and fitting into my father's budget, he once considered it as the household vehicle. Thankfully, my mother insisted that her family not drive around in a car nicknamed "a barbecue that seats four", and my father abandoned the idea. I thought this was wise of my mother until she also prohibited us from baking Shrinky Dinks in the oven, fearing they, too, could end in a fiery explosion.

With all this in mind, it doesn't change the fact that I am filthy and need a warm shower. Going with the premise that tires will ground you if a car gets hit by lightning, I put on my rubber flip-flops and hope they will serve the same purpose. I start the shower, and although it is warm, the water barely trickles out. This preserves a level of security since it's impossible to splash water on the exposed wires with this kind of shoddy pressure.

After dressing, I meet Rob outside on the veranda and ask him if he noticed anything while taking a shower. "Yes I saw it, but those things are okay to use. I read about them before we left."

"If they're safe, why do they call them suicide showers?" I reply. "Why not call them "Boy Ain't These Great" showers? They call it a suicide shower for a reason. Somebody somewhere got French fried with 220 volts."

"You're just being negative. Didn't you always say that's what you love about travel, you always get to experience a new way of doing things? Anyway, forget about that and take a look." I peek over the veranda and see the Pacific Ocean outstretched before me. It was so dark the night before we had no idea we were actually across the street from the beach. Through the palm trees, I see surfers coast across the waves and pitch up before wiping out. The cloudless sky cushions a fading image of a crescent moon, and breezes blow the fragrance of orchids in our direction.

We enjoy this peaceful moment before hearing a guttural roar coming from the hills behind us. It's the sound of howler monkeys bellowing across the treetops. These types of monkeys are the loudest land animal, and their voices can be heard from three miles away. They are one of the laziest monkeys and spend eighty percent of their existence lying in a tree, most likely doing Sudoku puzzles and gossiping with friends. At least that's what I would do if I had all that free time.

Tamarindo used to be a quiet fishing village but is now a bustling tourist destination. The town is located on a bay formed by Cabo Velas (Cape Sails), and the beaches to the north and south are nesting areas for the leatherback turtles that come to shore October through March. It is also one of the more famous places to surf, which is obvious by the large army of surfers marching down the street. I see one barefoot girl riding her bicycle while managing a board under her arm. She smiles at the other surfers as they all compare notes on the conditions of the waves. If they don't like them here, there are five other world-class surf breaks within driving distance.

We decide to get breakfast and walk down the main street that hugs the beach. Hotels and restaurants line the road as well as surf shops renting boards or offering lessons. I look up the hill behind us and see construction crews building houses and high-rise condominiums. Cement trucks are already on the road, kicking up dust as they drive to their work site. There is an explosion of growth occurring all around the town.

It's only seven o'clock but a few stores are starting to open their doors. We find a small cafe and order coffee with freshly baked croissants. We dig our feet in the sand as we sit at a patio table shaded by a palm tree. The waitress cheerfully brings out our food. The coffee comes with frothy, heated milk in a separate silver cup. It's a nice touch and greatly appreciated since I have been putting cold milk in my coffee for the past fifteen years. I take a sip and decide it's the best cup the world has ever seen. It is aromatic with a strong kick. The waitress tells me the beans are Arabica, grown at high altitudes in volcanic soil. This makes a superior product, and it is why Costa Rican coffee is one of the best in the world. It doesn't take long for me to finish and get a refill. The coffee alone is good enough reason to move here.

There is definitely a different rhythm to Costa Rica. You can see it on the faces of the people who walk past, and it is evident with the surfer's connection to nature. People are not in a rush. They take time to stop and talk with friends along the way. They look happy. In fact, everyone looks happy.

People walk the beach past the charred remains of coconut husks used for bonfires. Dogs run and splash in the ocean, only to sprint back and roll their soaked fur in the sand. It's amazing how quickly you can leave your problems behind when you are in this picture-perfect setting. The stress from my broken fax machine melts away as I watch a flock of pelicans fly over the surface of the ocean in silent formation. I would love to wake up to this every morning; sitting under a palm tree, eating breakfast, and watching the morning unfold.

My husband reaches for our rented cell phone (our cell phone from home will not work here) and calls our Costa Rican realtor, Martin. We decide to meet at his house, a ten-minute drive from Tamarindo. Rob picked him after making numerous calls to obtain information on buying real estate, and Martin was the only one who spent hours explaining the ups and downs of owning land here. Because of that attention, we chose him to show us properties.

We leave the beach and head back to the parking lot of the hotel. Our car is caked in dirt and mud from not only the roads but the rivers we had to drive through. Rob seems strangely content with the car's appearance, as if it is a testament to his great driving skills. As we head out of Tamarindo into the countryside, I can see why the trip getting here was so treacherous. The street resembles a war zone: craters so large you could crack an axle in them. It explains why I had such a bad headache the night before; the bumpy ride rattled my brain like a maraca. I am glad we paid extra for the bigger SUV with four-wheel drive. I am also thankful we did not have to take a bus here.

As we drive, I notice a large banyan tree sitting in front of someone's house. The tree starts out as a fig seed that germinates in the crevice of a host tree. It grows and becomes what is known as "the strangler fig," climbing up and around the host tree like a boa constrictor. The roots spread out laterally, covering most of the owner's yard. I am sure many children have played hide-and-seek in the deep chasms of this tree.

We continue past fields where horses and cattle graze in the sun. We slow down as an iguana leisurely crosses the road. Following the laid-back vibe here, even the iguana is not in a rush. We pull over when we see a family of howler monkeys in the trees. They jump from branch to branch letting out a loud warning once they notice us. There appears to be one big one in charge, and the rest follow his lead. It is an exceptional experience to see them in their habitat and not in a cage, especially considering a monkey once launched an unprovoked handful of excrement at me during Suzy Supalowski's fifth birthday party at Turtle Back Zoo. I learned at a young age that animals should never be kept in cages. I also learned not to stand in front of a monkey that has something other than a banana in his hand. But today the monkeys show no ill will; they turn around and go back to sleep.

Last night was difficult. There were times during the drive that I wanted to turn around, but I never imagined it would be this beautiful. And just like that, as my sister would say about childbirth, all the pain faded away. My life doesn't feel like a long dark tunnel anymore. Perhaps it's because I'm falling in love with a place I haven't been in for longer than twenty-four hours.

Martin the Incompetent Realtor

While in the car, I glance down at the Costa Rica real estate magazine on my lap and marvel at the homes listed. Clay colored tile roofs, spacious bright rooms, and nymphs dancing on fountains in the middle of circular driveways. I turn the page and see a home with an infinity edge pool that looks like it's cascading into the ocean view. I can't afford any of these homes, but it will be fun to walk through their open houses and imagine a white gloved butler pouring me a Cosmopolitan while I work on my tan. This daydream stops short when Rob pulls the car over on a dirt road. He parks in front of a field that leads up into a densely wooded mountain. There are no infinity pools in site.

Martin tells us the entire stretch of land is for sale; forty acres of forest situated on a steep incline. There is a spectacular panoramic ocean view only visible at the tippy top. This seems pleasant enough information, and I am waiting for Rob to start the car again and take me to the spectacular mansion that surely waits. Instead, both Rob and Martin get out of the car, go into the trunk, and take out three pairs of black galoshes. I put down my magazine. "What are you doing?"

"Hey... why don't we hike up the mountain and see what the view looks like at the top?" Rob answers. "It can't be more than a mile." He backs away and avoids making direct eye contact. His strategy when dealing with his wife is strikingly similar with how to avoid a bear attack.

It's clear why he is worried asking me this. My last cardiovascular activity occurred around 1998 when the sewer pipe exploded in the basement, causing raw sewage from the street to back into my house. I was on a three-hour bucket brigade, running back and forth from the backyard to the basement before reinforcements came and installed a new pipe. It was an incredible workout, and I would highly recommend it to anyone who is looking to burn calories and/or flirt with Hepatitis A. Since then, I've become happily sedentary, not performing any exercise that would pump my heart to any level of physical exertion. Other than the tachycardia sewage crisis, my heart has always officially beaten a steady rhythm of eighty beats per minute, the perfect zone for eating a bag of potato chips while reading real estate magazines. Precisely what I was doing before we pulled the car over.

The plan is to hike up the mountain, through dense vegetation, along an ambiguously marked path. I am not sure why Rob is willing to do this. "Maybe it's a good opportunity," he says. I think it is more like a good opportunity to get lost in the woods for six hours. The whole idea is crazy, but I don't have much choice. When I consider my fate sitting alone along the side of a deserted road versus contracting malaria while searching for my husband's "good opportunity," a mosquito-borne illness doesn't sound that bad.

Martin hands me my galoshes. I kick off my flip-flops and try on the pair of boots, only to find they are two sizes too big. To make matters worse, it's raining, and I don't have any rain gear except my travel-sized pink umbrella. I think back to the man on the plane wearing his all-weather hat and conclude I was a little hard on the guy. I unfold the umbrella, which provides a measly twelve square inches of coverage, making my Lilliputian purchase look more like a paper parasol garnish for a Bahama Mama cocktail. I lock my umbrella into place, and the metal frame rips through the top of the fabric, channeling rain directly onto the top of my head.

Martin goes first, then Rob, then me. Every time Rob walks past a plant, it snaps back like a taut rubber band at my head. On account of already being wet, I fold my umbrella and attempt to use it as a weapon against the vegetative onslaught. When the next branch springs toward my face, I hold up my umbrella for the pre-emptive block. The force of the branch smacking against my umbrella slingshots bugs, spores, and other forms of life into my face. A sticky cobweb now covers my mouth.

Slightly dazed and already confused, I follow my team and end up at the edge of a fast flowing river. Martin pauses, looks around the riverbanks, and walks straight through to the other side. I start to take off my galoshes, but he advises me to leave them on. He must have read the same article I did on river borne diseases in Costa Rica. I march through; however, the water quickly fills my galoshes, weighing them down like heavy sandbags. The water is now up to my thighs, and I am dragging my feet inch by inch to the other side. Once there, I empty my boots and find a crayfish; I toss him back into the river and watch him swim away.

We walk farther into the forest, my feet slipping and sliding as we go. I try to take another step, but my back leg is stuck in mud. I pull on my leg, but my foot leaves the boot, consequently stepping forward into a warm, muddy mass that squashes between my wet toes. My first impression is this feels pretty good. However, this soon turns into alarm as it becomes clear, by the warmth and the pungent smell, this is no ordinary pile of mud. I have no choice but to stick my stinky foot back into the boot and call out to my husband. "Rob, I think I stepped in..."

"What?" Rob yells as he keeps walking.

"I think I stepped in a pile of..."

"I still can't hear you."

"I think I stepped in a pile of shi......holy shit."

Martin stops short, and Rob bumps into him, causing me to crash into Rob. We are in the middle of a grassy clearing, equal distance from the forest behind us to the forest ahead of us. In the center are four bulls, big bulls, with sharpened horns perfect for gouging the awry traveler. I have literally stepped in a pile of bullshit.

I've never been this close to a bull before. They remain so still that for a moment I think they might be statues. That is until I see one of them flick a fly away with its tail. I decide that being so close to the bulls makes me equivalent to a rodeo clown. Only, I don't have a barrel to hide in.

"Maybe we should back up slowly. We can keep an eye on them that way. Do you think that's a good idea?" I whisper so as not to disturb even the tiniest gnats flying around their heads.

"I don't know, but I'm getting the hell out of here," yells Martin. He races through the clearing and disappears into the rainforest. Rob grabs my hand, and we both start running in the same direction. I toss my pink umbrella so that it doesn't provoke the bull like the red flag of a matador. We make it to the forest and find Martin hiding behind a tree. All three of us are gasping for air.

"I didn't know they would be there," pants Martin. His less than courageous actions have left me with little hope that the realtor can get us off this mountain. Nevertheless, we can see that the top is only a couple hundred feet away, so we carry on as if this ridiculous incident never occurred.

Once at the top, we are rewarded with a panoramic view of the Pacific Ocean. I find a rock to stand on and video tape the scenery. Martin starts his spiel about the potential for this property, and Rob is already running the numbers through his head. "If we charge one hundred thousand dollars a lot, times forty lots...that's like...that's like... a lot of money! We're going to be rich." I let Rob have his moment. I know he is smart enough to figure out that we are in the middle of nowhere and don't have a clue how to develop this land. My husband, with his sense of direction, wouldn't even be able to find this place again.

After we're done, we start the hike back down the mountain. We come across a large cactus, approximately thirty feet tall with each green stem about a foot in width. It seems oddly out of place in this rainy jungle environment. The five-inch long thorns poke straight out and are thick as porcupine quills. Rob stops in front of it and starts to poke at the green waxy stems in between the thorns.

Boing...Boing...Boing

"Hey guys look at this," Rob says.

"I don't think you should be touching that," I warn.

"This feels soooo cool," he replies. It's common for Rob to touch things and then eventually break the things he has just touched. I have seen the man shatter a priceless crystal wine glass after knocking it into someone's soup bowl at a dinner party. Once, at our neighbor Matt's house, Rob attempted to warm his feet by the new fireplace. However, he didn't see the closed glass doors because our obsessive-compulsive neighbor impeccably polished them. When Rob reached his foot toward the fire, he inadvertently pressed his sock-covered toe to the hot fireplace door, causing the fabric to burn and stick to the glass. No matter how much Matt tried to clean the scorched blemish, the impression of Rob's big toe remained plainly visible: a permanent fossil for future generations to behold. So I can get a little jumpy when I see my husband poking a cactus.

Boing...Boing.

He continues, but on his last poke, I hear a faint buzzing sound. "Shhhhh," I call out. Rob ignores me and keeps poking. "Seriously, stop it. Can't you hear that?"

"I don't hear anything. Lighten up and have some fun." But after his last poke, Rob pauses. We both hear a heavy buzzing coming from deep inside the thick green stem. We look up, and out from a crack shoots a darkness that develops into a villainous shadow above us.

"What *is* that?" I holler to Rob.

"I think it's a swarm of wasps."

"What do we do?"

"I don't know, but I'm getting the hell out of here," Martin yells. He takes off for the second time, disappearing into the brush. Rob grabs my hand and drags me down the mountain. My other arm flails widely around as I swat away the wasps; their synchronized buzzing resembles a high voltage electrical wire. Rob zigzags as if dodging bullets, but the wasps spot us at every turn. We finally outrun them and find Martin, not surprisingly, hiding behind a tree.

We are busy pulling twigs and leaves out of our hair when Martin reveals we are lost. We ran off the path, and he is unsure where we are. Our plan is to keep going down the mountain and find the same river we crossed an hour ago. If we continue past it, we should eventually find our parked car on the dirt road.

After thirty minutes, we approach a river, but it is not at the same place we crossed before and is much deeper. Unlike the last time, Martin doesn't look so eager to cross. He paces back and forth along the bank and scratches his head nervously.

"What's the problem?" I ask. "Can't you swim?"

"I can swim, but... ah... the water is deeper here, and I am a little concerned about crocodiles. Before, the river was shallow, and I wasn't too worried, but this is deep, and they can be anywhere." My blood pressure starts to surge. My husband looks at my reddening face and takes a couple steps back. I am about to attack.

"Okay, let's go over what both of you have put me through. I stepped barefoot in bullshit, which is still in between my toes. I ran up a mountain to get away from four bulls only to be chased back down the mountain by an army of wasps. So now I have to go back through a river I had already crossed, with the ever present fear of contracting a parasite, at a place where crocodiles could be waiting to eat me?"

"Hmm... yes... that's what I am suggesting," Martin mumbles.

In an anxious attempt to prove to me we are not in danger, Rob dashes into the river. The water quickly rises, climbing up to his neck, then his chin, and now over his mouth. He reaches his arms straight up holding the camcorder above his head. It reminds me of the scene in *The African Queen* when Humphrey Bogart's character gets out of his boat and drags it through a leech-filled swamp. Rob continues, holding his breath, walking until the water slowly recedes and I can finally see the back of his head again. He makes it out alive with a functioning camcorder and a leech-free body.

"It's under control. I'll help you get across," Rob says while wiping river gunk out of his eyes. But I don't need Rob's help because Martin and I find a shallow spot only six feet away, and it takes no time to join Rob on the other side.

"So should we put a bid in on this one?" Martin suggests.

I want to strangle him and throw him back into the water.

We gather ourselves and continue hiking down the mountain. I take one last look at the river and see something make a large splash. I don't bother telling the others, convincing myself it's just a really big fish. By the time we make it to the road, we are a half mile away from our parked car. The realtor, cheery and upbeat, now wants to show us a townhouse for sale. I am soaked through and look like someone who was just rescued from the jungle after a long and agonizing fight for survival.

I climb in the car and fasten my seat belt, wondering why we couldn't have looked at the townhouse first.

The Antipasto Cowboy

"Just think, maybe we'll run into Mel Gibson," Rob says while driving to Samara. Located an hour south of Tamarindo, Samara is a quiet beach town where I imagine I can find the movie star tanning on the beach or reading a script in a cafe (or in an uncontrollable fit of rage, but that's neither here nor there). Mel bought a ranch to get away from his stressful life in California. He frequents it often, and Rob is hoping this possible brush with celebrity will keep me in a good mood while we continue our quest. "We might even be invited onto his estate, wouldn't that be awesome?" he adds. He's right, the idea is splendid. I would engage Mel in lively conversation during this brief but magical moment: tell him I loved Lethal Weapon—"You were so believable playing Sergeant Riggs"—and ask if he, too, stepped in bull-shit while looking for property with his realtor.

We ended yesterday at the Hacienda Pinilla gated community. It was interesting walking through million-dollar townhouses while covered in river mud. I didn't acknowledge anyone's strange looks or whispers; I wore my dirt as a fearless badge of honor. After all, it's not every day that I get to walk around like Pig Pen. And it's not every day I get to drag that dirt across an imported marble floor.

Although it was fun to look at these townhouses, I have concluded that we will not be able to afford anything near the beach. Who would think that a little country in Central America could be so expensive? Moving here is not such a crazy idea after all, and plenty of people are doing it. Our realtor explains there are many of these expensive communities because Americans want to stay isolated. They do not want to intermingle with local people but would rather live behind big walls. There are more affordable places out there, and he insists he will find something perfect for us. Today we will check out another piece of land that is for sale with an ocean view. Martin promises I will not have to hike up a mountain to see it.

He gives Rob directions that lead us to a road bisected by a busy river. Martin wants Rob to drive through, but he hesitates, concerned he will stall in the middle. "You have four-wheel drive, for crying out loud. What are you waiting for?" Martin pipes in. I've just suggested we turn around when a red Nissan Sentra pulls up to the other side of the river. The man drives straight in, and we watch as the water quickly rises near to the top of his driver side door. He chugs along, but remarkably, the car doesn't stall. He makes it to our side and putts past us. We were one upped by a two door compact car.

"Told you so," Martin says. "This is Costa Rica; if you want to live here, you better get used to driving through rivers. So put it in four-wheel drive and let's go." Rob floors the accelerator like we're the A-Team, bouncing the car straight into the deepest part of the stream. Water flies everywhere, covering our SUV in mud as we make it to the other side. We now have an additional stratum on top of yesterday's crusty sediment. Our car is slowly becoming a paleontologist's dream.

Rob follows the directions to a piece of land that Martin promises will *blow your mind*. Rob is anxious for another adventure, but I am stuck on the fact that our middle-aged realtor uses the phrase *blow your mind*. The last time I heard this expression was in a Cheech and Chong movie. I'm starting to question a lot about Martin and have learned a few things these past couple days. He is forty-six, raised in California, and comes from a wealthy family. He is half-Mexican and half-Jewish, making me wonder if he had a mariachi band at his Bar Mitzvah.

Martin spent most of his life goofing off, but his family has stopped paying for his lifestyle, and he now he has to make his own living. He began selling real estate in Mexico and has moved south each year, now selling property in Costa Rica. I also picked up that he will not date any woman over twenty-five. According to Martin, women past twenty-five are a colossal pain in the ass. He goes on to explain this affliction only gets worse as women age. Martin says each year they become increasingly more bothersome, until at thirty, a woman is completely unfit to date. It's unfortunate that all the doddering women over twenty-five will never get the opportunity to date this prince charming.

Rob is still optimistic and has a fair amount of trust in the guy. "What about the fact that he left us in the rainforest, twice?" I asked Rob at the hotel.

"You just don't like him because he dates young women and runs around like a jerk for a guy his age. But what does that have to do with buying property?"

"Really Rob...twenty-five?"

"I'm not saying he should date your nieces, but he speaks Spanish, and without him what are we going to do, follow the dirt roads? We don't know where the hell we are."

"He's an idiot."

"If you're so smart, what realtor do you want us to use? How many phone calls have you made to Costa Rica?" He makes a point. I didn't orchestrate any of the planning for this trip. I should give Rob some credit for even finding this guy, but I can't help it that I am still annoyed. According to Martin, I am already over-the-hill in my mid-thirties. I have surpassed the "colossal pain in the ass" category and have fallen into the unseemly "completely unfit to date" division. This also explains why that cute surfer girl gave Martin the finger as we drove past. Unfortunately for her, she fits into Martin's dating criteria.

We drive up a long dirt road and see the owner of the land with his thirteen-year-old daughter, standing next to three horses. We get out and meet Hans, a bearish German who greets us with all the warmth and charisma of a Checkpoint Charlie border patrol. He owns the entire mountain that overlooks the Pacific Ocean, but the only way to view the land is on horseback. My startled expression immediately makes Rob uncomfortable, causing him to strike up an unsuccessful conversation with the German about currency exchange rates. Rob knows I've never ridden a horse and could not have anticipated my first one would be up a mountain in Costa Rica. I look at the three big horses and resign my fate to what is obviously ahead. Mel Gibson would never have put me in this position.

Rob rests his arm around my shoulders. "Don't be angry," he says. "You're not *hiking* up the mountain. This is going to be *sooo* great." (Whenever Rob gives me bad news, he always accentuates the word 'so'. He stretches it out; the longer he goes on, the more he is trying to convince me of an awful idea.) "This will be *sooooo* romantic: a horseback ride to the top, you and me together under the blue sky, the smell of the ocean in the air. You're okay, right? I mean... check out your horse; he looks like he's ready for the glue factory." He points to one eating grass. "You're lucky if you get it to walk up the mountain."

There are only three horses for four people. Just as I was going to volunteer to stay behind, Martin beats me to it. "Nadine, you've got to go up there and check out the view. I've seen it before, and it's great." Martin, the consummate realtor, makes his pitch from the safety of the air-conditioned car.

The mountain is a pleasant grassy landscape—not at all like the thick forest I had to hike through yesterday. But this won't be a beginners trail and is not the image I had of my first horseback lesson. Hans tosses me the reins.

"Take Mussolini; he's the slowest," he says and gives me the only horse that is having a bowel movement. I try to remain positive, knowing it's not every day I get to ride a horse named after a fascist dictator. "I would stay away from Heinrich; you have to know what you're doing to ride him." He turns to Rob, "You... you good with horses?"

"Yeah, of course, I rode them back in Brooklyn." Naturally, Rob thinks he is good at everything. I look over at Heinrich and watch as Rob tries to stick his foot in the stirrup. Rob's horse is a big, black stallion already shaking his head in irritation. Every time Rob attempts to put his foot in the stirrup, the horse takes a step forward. It's clear he doesn't want Rob to get on.

"I always wanted to ride a horse like this."

I wasn't aware of Rob's attraction to horseback riding. His prior experience was one short jaunt along the Belt Parkway eighteen years ago.

"Rob, you grew up over a Jewish deli in New York. Don't get ahead of yourself." I watch as he chases Heinrich in circles. "I don't think this is a good idea. And look, your horse won't even let you on. How do you expect to ride him up a mountain?" I glance over at Hans and lower my voice. "And for heaven's sake, you feel comfortable riding a horse named Heinrich? Because I don't feel so good riding a horse called Mussolini. *Mussolini*, Rob. You sensing a theme here?" Rob ignores me as he makes another attempt, hooks his leg into the stirrup, and hoists himself onto the saddle. Heinrich shakes his head and backs up toward Martin, who has already fallen asleep under a tree, most likely dreaming about all those lovely young shiksas who find him irresistible.

Hans leaps onto his horse like a professional jockey. "Komm mit mir," he yells. Rob's horse immediately follows but begins a jolty, sideways trot. It would be impressive if I didn't know Rob has lost all control at this point. I kick Mussolini, shout giddy-up, but he doesn't move. Hans circles back to me, but I'd rather he paid more attention to Rob's horse, who just took off down the road like Seabiscuit.

Hans and I ride side-by-side and meet up with Rob, who is already waiting at the base of the mountain trail. The trail is a meandering dirt path that zigzags up the steep mountain with sharp drop offs. The plan is to follow Hans along this gradual incline, back and forth, until we reach the top. Hans goes first. Rob's horse follows, but Mussolini lags behind, eating grass and blowing farts. I admire the lack of dedication in his performance.

It's not long before Heinrich starts snorting and jerking again. Rob attempts to pull on the reins, but the horse decides these traversing trails are too boring. He gallops up the sharp incline, bypassing the trail entirely and consequently dumping rocks and small boulders onto the trail in front of me. Heinrich continues until he and my Brooklyn cowboy are out of sight.

I carefully follow the trail until I meet the steepest part of the grade. I feel my hands slipping on the reins, so I lean onto the horse's neck and wrap my arms around him. I am too scared to look up as I bury my face into Mussolini's sweaty, flatulence-infused horsehair. I am two seconds from freaking out when we get to a small plateau and see Heinrich with Rob.

"What took you so long? Not bad, right?" Rob says as his shaking hands reach for a water bottle.

"Rob, you were completely out of control," I snap. Hans gets off his horse and ties Heinrich to a tree.

"Oh, we get off here?" asks Rob.

"No... *you* get off here."

"Huh?"

"You're too fat. I need you to get off the horse," Hans says.

"What? Right now? And leave me here?"

"That's right. It's not that much farther; you'll need to walk. The horse can't handle the strain," Hans answers. I don't even look at my pudgy husband as Mussolini and I abandon him on the side of the mountain.

I finally make it to the very top and peel my arms away from Mussolini's neck. Sweaty horsehair covers the right side of my face. I try to wipe it off, but the hair sticks to my skin. Ten minutes later, Rob emerges red-faced, sweaty, and out of breath. I ask him if he's okay, but he can't answer. He puts his hands on his knees and wheezes heavily. I start pouring water on his neck and pray he doesn't have a heart attack at the very top of the mountain.

"I guess everyone's alright then," he says between breaths. "Boy I hope *Heinrich* is doing okay." He takes a couple deep breaths and walks to the edge of the cliff. "Wow, this is a great view." Palm trees litter the landscape clear down to the ocean. They are evenly spaced out as if someone had already preplanned this magnificent view. It is more picturesque than the last piece of land we looked at. Since this is not a forest, it would be a whole lot easier to grade, but we still don't need an entire mountain, and Hans doesn't want to sell part of the land. It's all or nothing. Once again, Martin, the incompetent realtor, has brought us to a place that is too expensive.

It is beginning to get dark, and Hans asks us if we want to stay and watch the sun set.

"No," I tell him. "I want to go."

Hans allows Rob to ride down the mountain on Heinrich, but the minute Rob walks toward the horse, Heinrich starts smacking his hoofs and tossing his head back. Hans grabs hold of the reins while Rob climbs into the saddle.

As we travel back down the mountain, my horse takes a zigzag route, stopping occasionally to eat or have an extended toilet break. Rob's horse continues to kick and snarl in a constant tug of war. They wait for me, and all three of us ride under a canopy of trees. A gust of wind blows and tosses little red flowers from above onto our heads. Like a royal parade, the flowers continue to shower us while we ride under the branches. Costa Rica consistently has these moments: a day full of inconvenience followed by something so beautiful you would never consider leaving.

Once back on the road, Rob's horse struggles for control. He again side trots and ignores Rob's pull on the reins. Rob tries to get him back in line but Heinrich becomes increasingly agitated. Fearing he will be thrown from the horse, Rob lets up on the reins. A mistake, Rob learns too late, as the horse continues to pick up speed until he is at full throttle. It is becoming more apparent that the one horseback riding lesson he had on the side of the highway in Brooklyn was not adequate for the predicament he is facing now.

Rob can't seem to navigate the rhythm and finds himself crashing down into the saddle the exact moment when the horse is raising his back up. This action is tossing him almost two feet in the air with each stride. He drops the reins altogether and grabs onto the saddle.

"Whoa... Whoa," Rob screams as Heinrich races toward the tree Martin is sitting under. "Stop the horse! Stop the horse!" Rob calls out.

"No way, Man. I'm not going near that horse." Martin runs back another twenty feet as Heinrich dances in circles trying to kick Rob off. Hans catches up, dismounts his horse, and struggles to grab Heinrich. His thirteen-year-old daughter runs over and is able to calm the animal enough so that Rob can jump off. She then gets on and starts to ride the horse back to the stable.

"Man, what was your problem? That little girl is making you look bad," Martin laughs.

"You wouldn't even get off your ass and grab the reins to stop him," Rob barks. "I'd like to see you ride him back to the stable." Rob's love affair with Martin is beginning to dissolve. We leave the other horses tied to a tree and pile into our car.

We follow the girl and watch as the horse starts to trot sideways. She attempts to bring him back in line when he bolts, faster than he did with Rob riding him. She has lost all control, and we helplessly watch as she is tossed around. We speed behind in the car, approaching thirty miles per hour, when the horse careens forwards and kicks the girl off. She slingshots in the air and lands perfectly on her feet. Nadia Comaneci has nothing on this girl. Hans runs out of the car, for what I thought was to both console and congratulate her on her Olympic style athleticism, but he ends up screaming in German. She breaks into tears as he tells her to get back on the horse. She obeys him, jumps back on Heinrich, and cries all the way to the stable.

"If you don't get back on the horse, the horse wins," he explains. Spoken like a true dictator.

"Now that's tough love," Rob mumbles under his breath. This whole trip to Costa Rica is feeling like tough love. Before we drive away, a small plane flies overhead. I imagine Mel Gibson reclining in comfort while his private jet takes him to his ranch.

I am all but certain Mel didn't use Martin as his realtor.

Packing Up and Moving On

I'm bawling after giving away my potted ficus tree, a plant I unsuccessfully tried to kill for the past nine years. It was a gift from my husband while we were in chiropractic school. We'd just started dating, and it was a cute gesture since he didn't know that I am a notorious serial plant killer. I refused it water, denied it sunshine, and ignored its withering leaves as they fell off one by one on my living room floor. I all but poured gasoline on it, but this damn plant continued to live. It is now fifteen feet tall, and I am having a psychotic episode over giving it away to a stranger. There is no way I can take it to Costa Rica. This plan does not provide the luxury of holding on to any emotional crutches.

Let me put this in perspective. I live in a three thousand square foot house with hardwood floors, a television in the bathroom, and a giant fish tank in the wall, a house fit to be on *MTV Cribs*. I didn't cry when I sold any of this, but somehow this simple plant has reduced me into an inconsolable snotty mess. Rob doesn't ask what is wrong. He just brings me a grilled cheese sandwich, either to stifle or comfort me. Probably both.

After our many treacherous failures with Martin, we finally found a piece of property in Costa Rica. What's amazing is that we didn't have to hike or ride horses to get to it, no rivers to forge through. All it required was a drive up a mountain ridge onto a dirt lot—it took no more effort than that. Looking back, it is clear why Martin took us hiking and horseback riding to those ridiculously expensive pieces of property. Although we were not in the business of buying mountains, he was in the business of selling them.

Martin brought us to a beautiful development near Flamingo, Costa Rica. It's a smaller tourist town a half hour north of Tamarindo. While observing the mangroves, a dopey explorer named the area after mistaking a Roseate Spoonbill bird for a Pink Flamingo. The name apparently stuck. This piece of property suited us just right, with three building pads, each one giving a view to the Pacific Ocean. At ten thousand square meters, it had enough room for two houses and two pools. Rob even drew in the dirt where the pool should be positioned, giving the edge the illusion of cascading into the ocean. Back in New Jersey, few families had pools, and if you did, you were the coolest and most popular kid on the block. If I had a pool like the one Rob just drew, I would definitely be that kid.

I come from the oscillating sprinkler generation who spent summers running through fan shaped sprays of water shooting across our suburban backyards. My sister and I would do this for hours until my mother became concerned that jumping over a sprinkler didn't actually teach us how to swim. Her interest in our aquatic abilities coincidentally appeared after we pointed the sprinkler into an open dining room window and super soaked her drapes. As a result, we joined The Ashbrook Swim Club and had access to a large Olympic-sized pool with hundreds of other hot and sweaty children.

My sister and I often frequented their snack bar and bought Lucky Lights Cigarette Gum. There was never a cooler eight-year-old than one dangling a Lucky Lights from their recently chlorinated lips. It was the politically incorrect candy of my youth, paving the bronchial way for the next generation of tobacco enthusiasts.

As lame as my sprinkler was, my husband had it infinitely worse. His only relief from the heat was illegally taking a wrench to the corner fire hydrant and cranking it open. I only had my mother to contend with, but my husband had to run from the fire and police departments. Rob and his friends, much like *The Little Rascals*, would return an hour later and crank it open again.

Having a pool in the family would definitely establish that I'd made it. My dad would nod his head in approval, his youngest daughter living the high life. "No paid memberships here," he would say before we clinked champagne glasses and puffed away on our cigarette gum. He would of course ask me how much it cost, but I would flip my hand in the air and say, "If you have to ask, then you can't afford it." The problem with this plan, and one Rob and I haven't yet discussed, is if we bought the land, we could barely afford to build a house. What would be left over in our bank account would hardly cover anything more than a plastic kiddie pool.

Nevertheless, we did what most reasonable, educated people would do when considering buying property in a foreign country—we bought it on the spot. That's right, we forked over our hard-earned money for a deed in Spanish, a deed that could easily have been for an ice cream stand in El Salvador. Except for stealing my dad's Eldorado when I was seventeen and crashing it five minutes later, I never did anything as incomprehensible and irresponsible as this. I hated my job so much I was willing to believe documents in a language I didn't understand.

Now we are selling or giving away all our possessions and tossing our lives away as if they were an overfilled Hefty garbage bag. You know you have too much stuff when you own a robotic hamster that sings *Kung Foo Fighting* while swinging little plastic nun-chucks. At one time, I thought this purchase made perfect sense. However, I am now contemplating what could have motivated me to walk out of the store with a singing mechanical rodent. Over the years, I lapsed into an irreversible form of shopping dementia to compensate for the fact I was exhaustively miserable.

This form of endorphin pumping therapy got me in trouble in the past. In graduate school, I racked up a two thousand dollar credit card bill at Ann Taylor. I had to rent a cheap basement apartment without heat so I could use the remainder of my financial aid money to pay off the debt without anyone finding out. Now that I had a good paying job, my addiction emerged once again, finding a safe haven by anonymously shopping off the QVC channel. I never considered I was out of control since I had a patient who bought her hot dogs from QVC. *What nut would buy her hot dogs off QVC? Surely I'm not like her,* I thought as I ordered a year's supply of pumpkin scented candles. Item number A-14234. And let's not forget the fur coat debacle.

I'm discovering that doing inventory of one's stuff can really be a reflection of how happy or unhappy one is. How could I have possibly acquired so much? And how could my life feel so oddly empty at a time when I have more possessions than ever before? It's bizarre that I felt happier in college when I owned so little. Owning less junk gives you a freedom that you don't realize exists until you have a house filled with things you constantly need to care for (even the Kung Foo hamster had to be dusted every once in a while).

Never once did I wrap anything in newspaper or bubble wrap when I moved from one dorm room to the next. I didn't even own a set of luggage to shove anything in. I threw most things into pillowcases or milk crates before tossing them into my sister's orange 1977 Cadillac Coupe Deville, a car rivaling the gas guzzling quality of the Hays family Chevy Impala. The Cadillac's glove compartment alone was roomier than most compact cars on the road today. And the trunk space? Well... let's just say no wonder John Gotti drove a Cadillac.

When furnishing my apartment, those same milk crates were perfect as end tables, TV stands, hampers, stools, and the occasional footrest. Milk crates were the *piece de resistance* of multi-functional furniture. It just didn't make sense to commit to items you really didn't want or need. Now, I own enough table settings to host a banquet for the Queen of England, and what's more ridiculous is that I have yet to invite one person over to my house for dinner.

Now it all has to go, and I'm bawling over that ficus tree. Rob's attitude has been consistent throughout this process. He goes about his daily activities with a smile, completely unaffected that we might have made the biggest mistake of our lives. I am terrified—pain down the left arm and "power up the defibrillator paddles" kind of terrified. I have undone everything that I worked for all these years, just like that. I threw my money away for a piece of dirt in a foreign country, and all my husband can say is, "Do you know where I put my guitar pick?" Classic Rob.

How did my parents handle the news? I would have received a better response if I'd told them I was interviewing for the senior operative position in Al Qaeda. My mother, always appreciating a job with benefits, would have defended me to my father, "But Bill, she met with *the* Abdulla Yusuf Maktab Mohamed, and he guaranteed her a medical plan with dental, *dental* insurance, for Christ's sake." But revealing I am leaving to bum around Central America has practically put them in the ICU. The other day, I saw my mother order two burial plots. I'm not sure if they were for her and dad or for Rob and I. Everyone is angry with me, especially my niece, who threw a Sesame Street sippy cup at my head.

"Do you have to sell the house?" my parents ask. "Why don't you keep it so you have something to come back to?" No, I need the money for the move, and I can't come back. I sold my practice, and according to the non-compete clause, I can't work as a chiropractor here for five years. I was happy to sign it and get the practice sold. After the new owners slid me my check, I felt like ripping off my scrubs and doing a table dance on top of the attorney's conference table. I imagined tossing my patient files around like one dollar bills to the Motley Crue song *Girls, Girls, Girls*. I was that ecstatic. It was the first time, in a long time, I was that happy. However, that feeling did not last long, and the sense of uncertainty kicked in when I realized my life was going to change drastically.

So sorry, Mom and Dad, I'm quitting my job and moving to Costa Rica, but first Rob wants to drop by Zurich, Switzerland.

Swiss Banks, Gassy Water, & Killing Your Spouse

"What could you possibly know about Swiss Banks?" I ask Rob while he stands in his underwear. "And it's three in the afternoon; are you going to put on pants today?"

"Think about it: we will not have an address in the States, and we can stash our money in any bank in the world. *Anywhere.* Why not at least entertain the idea? And the answer to your second question is... maybe I'll wear pants, maybe I won't. No need to commit either way."

Ever since Rob stopped working, he also stopped shaving and wearing pants. This concerns me because we have no curtains on our living room windows—all the more problematic because the school bus stops in front of our house.

"Besides, I met with a financial planner, and he said if we move our money into a Swiss bank, we don't have to pay taxes on it."

When I think of Swiss banks, what comes to mind are vaults of gold bars, strange foreign bond certificates, and secretive transactions behind closed doors. Nowhere in my imagination has the argument *Why was my debit account charged a thirty-cent fee at Arby's?* been debated in the hallowed halls of a Swiss bank. The exact dispute I had the luxury to take part in with my bank this past week.

"You realize you haven't signed a check in ten years. Do you think it's magic that all the bills get paid?"

"I seem to recall you making one of your 'executive decisions' to take care of all our banking," Rob says.

"That's because I used to find moldy insurance checks under the refrigerator, but I wouldn't mind going to Europe, mostly because I'd love to see you try to pull this one off."

I am certain there is no way a Swiss bank will speak with us, but I plan to make the most out of this trip. I want to try two things Swiss related: yodeling and eating generous amounts of cheesy fondue (all the while pretending to be a distinguished socialite). I'll even ask for a room with a bidet: a geyser of warm luxury rarely embraced by the American consumer, and something I probably won't need after eating all that fondue. This will be our last trip before moving, so I might as well live it up, even if constipated, in Switzerland.

Switzerland has quite an interesting history, notably during WWII. They cozied up with the Nazi's, ultimately becoming the Laverne & Shirley of global domination. Like true BFF's, they each enjoyed the other's company, one working diligently on their "final solution," the other laundering the looted gold in their banking system. After the war, the Swiss refused to return the stolen money, and it took close to fifty years for the truth to unfold. A 1.25 billion dollar settlement was awarded to the victims in 1998. With all this bad press, I wonder if it's bad taste to ask whether the Third Reich got free checking with their account.

A week later, we land in Zurich, the wealthiest city in Europe with close to the best quality of life. It is so clean and beautiful I wonder why we don't live here. That is, until I buy a frankfurter from a street vendor for seven dollars. Case closed. But despite the expensive food, they do offer free bicycles and maps to tour the city. Rob takes one and circles the banks he wants to visit: four in total. I'm busy trying to figure out why my bike looks like it's built for Andre the Giant. It has come to my attention that the Swiss are a strapping lot. It's surprising their humongous fingers don't get in the way when making all those cute little timepieces and Swiss army knives.

I lower my seat as far as I can, but I still can't touch the ground. It feels like I'm a kid again, trying to ride my sister's ten-speed Schwinn. Rob hops on his bike and takes off down the street. I have no choice but to follow, peddling my stubby legs as fast as I can. He turns toward Bahnhofstrasse, a famous shopping district filled with high-end stores bordering the street. Electric passenger trams zoom back and forth, sharing the road with bicyclers and pedestrians. Their deep metal grooves in the ground are difficult to avoid while peddling, criss-crossing in dizzying patterns throughout the length of the street.

"I can see the bank; it's to the left," Rob yells out. I'm glancing behind to check and see if a tram is coming when both my wheels get stuck in the grooves. I fall over and crash my bike in a spectacle rarely seen outside the last stage of the Tour de France— except I did it on one of the most glamorous streets in the world. Spinning wheels fan what's left of my pride as Rob lifts me and the bike off the ground. Eating asphalt seems all the more embarrassing in front of women carrying Prada bags.

We lock the bikes in front of the bank and walk into a Carrera marble masterpiece. The building has granite countertops, glossy floors, and an atrium three stories tall. It's all nauseatingly intimidating. We walk straight to the front desk, where Rob asks to see someone about opening an account. The woman raises an eyebrow, proceeds to raise both when looking at the gravel in my hair, and explains that to open an account you must have fifty thousand dollars.

"I have that amount," Rob says. She then lifts a black receiver and dials a number. She whispers something in German and hangs up.

"Sir, you vill need one hundred thousand dollars to open an account."

"I have that; can I please talk with someone?" Rob urges. This charade continues until the minimum deposit increases to a quarter of a million dollars. Rob raises his hand in the air and yells, "I GOT IT! Please, I want to speak with someone immediately." She stares at Rob, waits a few more seconds, and gets back on her black phone.

"Someone vill be down to assist you," she mutters.

We back away and wait by an elevator. "Wasn't that fun?" Rob whispers to me. "Can you believe it? We're going to meet with a Swiss bank representative."

"I can't believe you're pulling this off. Why did you tell them we have that much money?"

"Just play along. We're not doing anything illegal, so don't get worried," Rob smirks. We watch the blinking numbers above the elevator decrease. 5...4...3...2...DING. The doors open to a 6'5", smashingly good-looking man. These Swiss are really, really huge.

Nicholas Bielmann greets us as we join him in the elevator. He takes a card and sticks it into a slot before pushing the fifth floor button. I admire the security precautions and wonder what is so wonderful about the fifth floor. As the doors open, a dazzling blonde woman meets us. She reminds me of Heidi Klum, and I can't imagine why she is working in a bank and not modeling couture clothing on some runway in Paris. Nicholas excuses himself as Anna escorts us to a private room. (Of course, *Anna*, never Agnes or Bertha. Pretty girls always have pretty names.) She turns and escorts us down a long hallway lined with steel doors on both sides. With her high heels echoing against the surrounding marble, I notice she does not have one crease in her black Armani suit. I notice many in my Old Navy cargo pants.

The hallway continues for what must be the span of two buildings. She opens a door on the right and leads us into a small conference room. Rob and I take seats at opposite ends of the table.

"I vill bring you beverages. Gas or no gas?" Anna asks. What? Is this some kind of joke? I glance at Rob, and he doesn't know what to say, either. I fidget in my seat and decide when presented with a question that could be misconstrued for farting, it is always best to go for the 'no gas' selection.

I have to admit, I am feeling pretty important right now. My husband is amazing. I knew I married a crafty city boy, but this goes to show he can do anything.

"Now this is how a bank should treat their customers," I whisper to Rob.

Suddenly, I hear a grinding noise and see the awning outside the window move automatically as the blinds rise inside. They apparently adjust accordingly to the angle of the sunlight, so very James Bond.

Anna returns with chocolates and bottled water on a silver tray. The water is what she meant by gas or no gas. When she leaves, Rob reaches for the chocolate, and I take a few pictures. It occurs to me: if this room is so sophisticated there might be a hidden camera somewhere. Now they caught me taking a picture of no gas water and the automatic awning, just the clients they were hoping for.

"Sorry to keep you waiting," Nicholas says as he enters the room. He lays his leather briefcase on the table and pops open each snap. "How can I assist you today?"

Rob explains he wants to open a bank account.

Nicholas seems eager and says the paperwork is simple and straightforward— that's until he hears we are from the United States.

"That changes things significantly," he says after taking a deep breath. "There are several options regarding a specific form that Americans should fill out."

Rob clarifies to Nicholas that we will be living in Costa Rica and don't have to fill out this tax form.

"To be honest, I am not clear with the US tax code, so I will call up a tax specialist to answer our questions." He gets up and leaves the room.

I begin to get nervous and wonder why we need to talk with someone else. However, it does give me a chance to pocket the wrapped chocolates Anna brought us.

A few minutes later, the "specialist" walks in wearing Dragnet sunglasses. He stands over Rob and explains that this form will go straight to the US government, notifying them we have an account in Zurich. He slides the form to us and leaves the room. I sneak the chocolates back on the table just in case this guy is waiting for me outside.

It is becoming clear that we will have to pay Federal taxes, regardless where we live or where we earn our money: the exact opposite advice from what the financial planner had told my husband. I am wondering if Rob got this information from his Brooklyn "bookkeeping" buddy, Frankie Two Fingers.

"So, you don't have to sign it... most Americans don't... the US tax laws are so complicated." Nicholas takes the form off the table.

"But your colleague said it was illegal," Rob returns.

Nicholas shifts in his seat. "No, he never said the word *illegal*."

Now Rob shifts in his seat.

I didn't do any of my own research and don't know what to say.

Thankfully, Rob gets up and ends the meeting, telling Nicholas we are late for our next appointment. Nicholas hands us a copy of our application and says he will open an account for us and we can fund it later.

"That guy was skating around something," Rob says as we exit the bank. "You can't bullshit a bullshitter." He unlocks our bikes, and we ride across town to the second bank. Maybe this will go better.

The next bank is equally if not more impressive than the last. Once again, we are escorted to a private room. I look out the window and see St. Peter's church, famous for the biggest clock face in Europe. I turn around and walk toward a painting on the wall.

"Holy crap, this is a Picasso," I tell Rob. "I can't believe it... look... I'm touching it."

I'm running my fingers along the frame when a woman walks in with crackers and small wrapped mints. I ask for gassy water this time, just to shake things up a bit. William Fenstermacher, an older banker, walks into the room and introduces himself. He begins the initial proceedings of opening an account. Rob brings up the tax form and asks, once again, if we have to sign it.

William leans back in this chair. "Let me explain it to you this way," he says while wrapping his hands behind his head. "If you are a terrorist...don't sign it. If you are a drug smuggler... don't sign it. If you are a man who wants to kill his wife... hmm... don't sign it."

I choke on my gassy water. Nothing like talk of murdering one's wife to get me to sit up and pay attention.

"But we are not any of those. So you are telling us we should sign it?" Rob says, easing my suspicions.

"No," William says. "I am not saying that." Rob and I are both confused whether to sign it or not. I can sense the banker can't believe how naive we are. I can't believe the option of killing your wife is a decision factor on whether one should open an account.

"Speaking of terrorists," Rob says, "if they nuke Zurich, how will I be able to access my money? Since there are no bank statements that come with this account, how will I know my money is safe?"

This practically makes William fall out of his seat laughing.

"Is a Swiss bank safe? You've got to be kidding. Why would the terrorists nuke Zurich when we have their money here?" Wow. I didn't see that one coming.

Instead of letting it go, Rob digs deeper.

"Yeah, well, what if our president finds out you are harboring the terrorists' money? That can't be good for international relations."

"Once again, why would he do that when we have his money, too?" Wow, this is about as uncomfortable as it gets. I want to get up and leave, but William slides over a piece of paper.

"Now this you must fill out. It is a record of a relative that we can reach if your account becomes inactive for ten years... or you drop dead... whichever comes first."

"I thought a Swiss bank account was anonymous and secretive? Just an account number with no name attached."

"Well, the government has made us change some procedures." William leans in and whispers, "You know, because of the whole Jew thing."

Okay, have a great night, thanks for coming, tip your waitress on the way out. I should be out yodeling... eating fondue... crashing my gigantic bike in front of Swarovski Crystal... anything but discussing ways to launder money in a Swiss bank. I feel like we ventured into information that I didn't want or need to know. This proves I could never be a spy. I am already wiping sweat off my forehead and feel a facial tic coming on. How did Mata Hari do it? Then again, she was convicted and consequently executed by firing squad, all the more reason to get the hell out of here. We get up to leave, and William explains, just like Nicholas, that he can open the account for us and we can fund it later.

The third bank is on the other side of town, so we bike the scenic route along the Limmat River. Bright red and yellow flowers bloom in long concrete planters, and people are walking hand in hand enjoying the sunshine. My nerves relax as the cool air clears my head. There are only two more banks I have to contend with before Rob will give up.

At the third bank, Christian Weiss greets us. He is the youngest of the bankers and reminds me of a reincarnated Cary Grant. We start with the bank accounts, and Rob asks, for the third time, if we should sign the tax form.

Christian just shrugs his shoulders and looks at his watch.

"I think we should talk about this over lunch. Don't you?"

"But we have another bank appointment in half an hour," Rob replies.

Christian laughs, "There is no such thing as a half hour lunch in Switzerland." Once he offers to put it on his expense account, with us not wanting to share another seven-dollar frankfurter, we decide to blow off the next meeting and join him.

We walk along the river until it meets Lake Zurich. Christian points to a busy outdoor restaurant filled with businessmen in varying shades of black suits.

"This is where many bankers lunch," Christian says as we are lead to a table with a lake view. He lights a cigarette, leans back, and blows the smoke overhead into the yellow umbrella shading the table. The smoke swirls up the handle and lingers in the umbrella before a cool breeze whisks it away. The risk of emphysema never looked so attractive.

Rob tries to talk business, but Christian is too busy checking out women jogging along the water. He is less interested in our banking needs and more interested why we came to Zurich in the first place. We order our insanely expensive lunch and spend the next two hours talking about ourselves.

He listens carefully as we tell him our plans to move to Costa Rica. Christian seems impressed and tells us he would like to do it, too, but he rarely works more than an eight hour day, gets two hour lunches, four weeks' vacation time a year, and excellent health insurance. The biggest problem he has is whether he will vacation on the French or Italian Riviera. Why in the world would he want to move?

Three hundred dollars later, we leave while Christian turns to light a cigarette for a beautiful woman. From the back, she looks like Anna, but we don't hang around long enough to find out if Christian's flirting was successful. I wouldn't bet against him. I'm sure his charisma rarely fails him.

This experience was by far the highlight of the trip. I eventually went on and ate fondue on a narrow cobblestoned street, yodeled on Mount Pilatus, and enjoyed a hotel room in Lucerne with a bidet.

Once home, Rob admits that the small amount of taxes we have to pay per year makes it ridiculous to even think about moving our money to Switzerland.

"We actually didn't even have to go," he confesses.

We ended up opening three Swiss bank accounts and funding none of them.

It doesn't surprise me that Rob's idea did not turn out as planned. They rarely do, but I am glad I went on this trip. There are many things you can forget about a vacation, and I am sure the memories of Switzerland will eventually fade. But I will always recall the time I drank gassy water, under a Picasso, in a Swiss bank.

A Dog and Cat on a Mission

"Walk through again, Sir," the TSA agent orders.

Rob backs up through the metal detector with the pet carrier, but it still beeps.

"You need to take the cat out of the bag," the man says while radioing additional backup.

Pumpkin, my fat and hairy cat, is being detained as a possible explosive threat. Newark Liberty Airport is at a standstill. I am watching all this as I pick my suitcase up off the conveyor belt. Passing through security was a breeze for me, but poor Rob is being hassled like he's the shoe bomber.

Rob reaches in the bag and pulls out our junkie cat. A week before the trip, my veterinarian gave me pills to drug him during the flight. "It'll just relax him," she said. This morning I slipped him one, and my once alert cat now looks like Courtney Love on a Saturday night. His eyes are half closed, and he can barely lift his head. I just ruffied my kitty.

What the vet didn't tell me, and a side effect I never considered, was the possibility of incontinence. Now Pumpkin has ungraciously peed all over himself, soaking the pet carrier. All this wouldn't have been the biggest deal if Rob didn't have to walk through the metal detector with Pumpkin pressed to his chest.

Beep...Beep...

"Walk through again," the agent demands as urine permeates Rob's T-shirt.

The people in line behind him start to get impatient as more agents come to inspect the suspicious cat that is trying to board a plane. The same people are now getting a whiff of what is happening ahead of them and wisely take a few steps back.

It occurs to me that I put a collar around his neck with a metal identification tag; however, he is so fuzzy, no one can see it past his fur. I walk toward Rob, but a two hundred and fifty pound woman with her arms crossed in front of her chest stops me. She just stands there, blocking me from helping Rob. I judge the situation, go over all the options in my head, and after remembering the pummeling I got by a girl just her size in high school, I decide to go to the food court and get a pretzel at Aunt Annie's. I convince myself it's what Rob would have wanted me to do—save myself and remember him in happier times.

"There you are," Rob says after I return. He stuffs Pumpkin back in the carrier and zips up the bag. "Oh good, you got a pretzel." It's amazing how cheery he is after causing half a dozen people to miss their flights. He grabs a clean T-shirt from his carry-on and changes while sitting in the massage chair outside the Brookstone store. Rob's never one to be concerned about privacy.

Luckily, all the chaos did not do much to wake Pumpkin. He continues to remain in a hazy coma, surely dreaming of butterflies and catnip scented litter boxes. There are a few pills still in my pocket if he needs another, or if I want to be knocked out, too. I've never tried it before, but after looking at how relaxed Pumpkin is, popping a Quaalude and peeing oneself looks like an excellent way to fly.

Unfortunately, my dog can't have the drug since she must remain alert as she boards the cargo hold. This thought made me so sick that last night I looked up every way a dog could die on a flight. My husband found me crying all over the computer keyboard as I mumbled the odds of Clementine making it to Costa Rica alive, exactly the disposition my husband was hoping I would be in the night before our trip.

Rob knew I could never leave without my pets, so we needed a house that would rent to pet owners. A couple weeks ago, we traveled back to Costa Rica to find a place where we could leave a security deposit and first month's rent. We chose not to go back to Flamingo where we bought our property but to a town called Grecia. Since we will need to buy a car and work on our residency process, it seemed logical to start in a town that is only an hour away from the capital. It is also an area known for having dozens of car lots and would be the perfect place to start car shopping. We give ourselves a year to get all the essentials done before moving to the beach and building on our lot.

We met with a realtor who found us a great place for four hundred and fifty dollars a month: a two-bedroom, two-bathroom house in a gated community with only two other homes in the entire complex. The Valley Ranch Development backs up to a forest reserve, and from the house, you can't see any of the neighbors. I never lived in such seclusion. My neighborhood growing up had identical little houses, one right next to the other. There was no privacy, and all the tiny backyards aligned with everyone else's. My husband lived in apartments and didn't even have a backyard. His mother still does not like to step on grass, something she finds dirty and filled with bugs. There is a lot of grass in Costa Rica, and I will remind my mother-in-law of this when she wants to visit.

When we stood on the porch with the realtor, all we could hear were birds and the waterfall behind the house. The sound of the river had a hypnotic effect, so peaceful and calming that Rob and I knew this would be the best place to start our new life. To live surrounded by acres of forest would give us a new perspective, and a place to trade the years of stress for the sound of the wind passing through the trees.

Plus, I think it's good that Rob can walk around in his underwear while playing his guitar and no one will see him.

Our plane boards early, and I scoot to the window seat. I watch the conveyor belt to see if Clementine is being boarded, but all I see are the men tossing the luggage into the plane. Rob seems relaxed. Besides the cat pee, he is happy and can't wait to get to Costa Rica. Nothing bothers Rob too much when we travel. He always remains calm and capable, even if the plane is delayed or our baggage is lost. He is probably the best traveling partner I ever met, a fact I am more than qualified to state.

In my twenties, I went with my college boyfriend on a trip to California and got the chicken pox. As my fever peaked at 103°F, he dumped me in a hotel room and disappeared for twelve hours with a group of people he just met. For dinner, his culinary gift to me was a half-eaten McDonald's Egg McMuffin that smelled like the back seat of the Hertz rental car. It was that defining moment when I knew I could never spend the rest of my life with this jerk, something I should have known sooner after hearing his Andrew Dice Clay impressions at my family's Thanksgiving dinner.

My husband could relate to my California disaster. When he was in his late teens, he earned money cleaning boilers in the projects. He saved enough to take his girlfriend with him to the Bahamas. It was his first trip outside Brooklyn, and he was anxious to get in the clear water and snorkel along the reefs. His girlfriend, on the other hand, wanted to sit in the recreation room and make macramé friendship bracelets. He found out she didn't like the beach, or the ocean, or doing any activity that didn't involve an arts and crafts project. So he snorkeled and played in the ocean alone for the entire week while using his disposable underwater camera to record every moment. The best part of the story is when they broke up, she kept all the underwater pictures because they meant too much to her. In return, she gave him a friendship bracelet.

Knowing someone is not the same as knowing someone while sick with chicken pox in San Francisco. Instead of pre-marriage counseling, I believe sending an engaged couple on a trip is more helpful. Traveling before getting married could cut the divorce rates by eighty percent; I am convinced of it. Rob and I are a good match, which is something that is important if you love to travel and even more of a necessity if you plan to move across the globe.

Rob has really made this move as easy on me as possible. The past six months could have been a tsunami of headaches and arguments, but he handled everything calmly, except for when he became sick.

Rob became seriously ill when he started throwing up and couldn't stop. Who knew you could actually puke yourself to death? After tossing around a bunch of horribly serious diagnoses, he ended up having an odd nerve disorder. Stress can set it off, and Lord knows there had been a lot of that over the years. Rob said work was killing him, and he was right. The one good thing that came from the nights by his hospital bed was that it didn't make a difference what anyone thought about the move to Costa Rica. It became crystal clear that Rob could not continue working like this. The choices we'd made about our lives were our own and no one else's business. So with that, I chose not to question our decision anymore, never to doubt myself or the reasons why we're doing it. From now on, there is no turning back.

Pumpkin barely wakes up during the five-hour flight. I can hear little moans, but nobody notices. Even as we land, he picks his head up only to fall back asleep. He stays like this all the way to the baggage carousel. I hold on to him as Rob grabs the luggage, one by one, until he fills the entire perimeter with our bags.

This was the first trip Rob did the packing, consequently devoting two suitcases entirely to tools. He packed so many screwdrivers and drill bits it looks as if we are building our own strip mall. Rob even packed two large winches with one hundred feet of steel twine just in case our car needs to be cranked out of a ditch. After we account for all our bags, I go to the desk to request my dog, where a young man with an airport ID tag meets me.

"You looking for dog?" he asks.

"Yes, where can we get her?"

"Oh, I have her. She okay, but papers take long time. Very long... can take so long."

"Please, can we have our dog back?" I plead.

"I can try to speed things... hmm... I can try... but..."

"How much?" Rob demands. He doesn't waste any time with this guy. Rob immediately understands that this guy wants a bribe, and that if we don't give it to him, he will find a way to hold our dog until we acquiesce.

"Thirty dollars, and I help you," the man says while smiling nervously.

Many people might balk at this. They might say that the principle of the matter is I should not be bribing to get my dog back. On the other hand, I have no idea if my dog is alive. And if she is, she desperately needs to get out of that crate. Instead of arguing any longer, we pay the man the thirty dollars and he wheels out our dog. He passes through customs without even showing the specially stamped vaccination papers I needed to transport my pets internationally. Thankfully, Clementine is alive, albeit scared. My cat is slowly waking up and has started swatting at imaginary moths in his carrier.

It's now ten o'clock, dark, and raining. We get a taxi to the rental car company and rent a roomy van. It is the only vehicle that can fit the dog crate, eight suitcases, and a smelly cat. We know we will have to come back and return it tomorrow for something cheaper, but for now, it will have to do. I am responsible for navigating us back to Valley Ranch, so I keep an eye out for landmarks on where to turn. Grecia, like every other town in Costa Rica, does not have any street signs.

After getting lost for twenty minutes in a country where I don't know the language, in the middle of a rainy night, somehow I get us home. We drive through the gates and pass two houses before finding the one we rented. We get the animals out of their crates and bring the suitcases into our new home. Finally, this is it. We made it. We are officially starting our new life tonight, and I plan to squeeze every drop out of this experience.

Part II

Pink Houses, Clouds, & Crazy People

T he past few days we've been busy unpacking and enjoying the tranquility. Not being disturbed by car horns, leaf blowers, and radios is sending me into sensory detox. I am actually experiencing a much anticipated lifestyle withdrawal. This withdrawal is accompanied by a less than anticipated loss of electricity. Sometimes it flickers on and off, while other times it just stays off for eight hours. The realtor didn't tell us that the higher you go on the mountain, the more likely you will have trouble with your electrical lines.

Upon further investigation, Rob discovers the wires in the house are not grounded properly. During a thunderstorm, all the outlets pop, making us run around unplugging everything. The thunder also makes the phone ring, which is nice since it gives the illusion I have lots of friends calling me. Even though we have these electrical issues, the good news is we don't have a suicide shower. I can shave my legs without electrocuting myself, something I am sure I will write in all my Christmas cards this year:

Dear Mr. and Mrs. Finklestone,

Costa Rica is enchanting. I wash my hair by candlelight and have yet to be struck with several hundred volts of electricity.

God Bless Every One

My daily walks with Clementine up and down the mountain give me the opportunity to snoop around the development. Rumor has it the investors couldn't build anymore because the municipality refused additional permits. This is now protected land, and it looks as if there will be no more construction. One of the houses I call the Barbie Dreamhouse because it has a funny pinkish stucco facade and looks like it's around ten thousand square feet. No one lives there. I walk past it every day and stick my head in between the wrought iron gates to see if there is any activity. If there is someone, I'm sure they are sick of me doing this, but so far, the house looks empty.

Jim, the Jehovah's Witness, owns the second house. I know his name is Jim, but occasionally he changes his name to Rodger. I never know which one to say, so I just address the guy as "hey you" when I see him. Last time we met, he told me Armageddon was coming. I quickened my pace and ate two ice cream sandwiches when I got back to the house. I thought it was a good time to indulge, considering pre-Armageddon calories never count.

Jim/Rodger works for the church on the Caribbean side of Costa Rica and only comes back to the house a few times a year. He has absolutely no furniture in his house. I know this because he has absolutely no curtains on his windows. Rob thinks I'm nosy, but how can I avoid looking at his house? It's on my way to the Barbie Dreamhouse, where I confess to my voyeurism. I explain to Rob that in some circles my behavior would be considered community watch. I would be applauded for my conscientious attention.

Rob just looks at me and tells me another Brooklyn story of someone getting stabbed in the head for being an undesired witness to something. He is never at a loss for these kinds of stories; some involve ice picks, while others are with sharpened screwdrivers. I sit down and listen to him like it's a twisted after school special. He continues to lecture me like I'm his teenage daughter asking for the keys to the family car.

Since we are near the top of the mountain, we are at a higher altitude than the rest of the town. At the same time every afternoon, a cloud rolls in passing through the screens, under the doors, and taking over the house like a deadbeat third roommate. Rob thought the air was refreshing, so he opened all the windows to let the cloud float inside the house. After a couple of hours, it drifted away, leaving a layer of condensation on the walls, doors, and furniture. This condensation then turned into a layer of green mold on the walls, doors, and furniture. That explains our discovery of two cans of anti-mold Pledge under the kitchen sink. The good news is this will only occur in the rainy season. The bad news is a can of anti-mold Pledge costs ten dollars here.

What is it like living in a cloud forest? Not to sound snarky, but there is no other way to describe it—cloudy. While you are watching the television, you do it through a cloud. Doing a Sudoku puzzle? Yep, you're trying to see the numbers through a cloud. I have to say, it's kind of cool. If you had said I'd be living in a cloud a couple months ago, I would have thought you were crazy. But here I am, walking my dog in a cloud. Quite a heavenly experience.

Another fun thing about living here is Carlos, the caretaker of the development. I can usually find him cutting acres of grass with a weed whacker in an apron and hood ensemble that makes him look like a beekeeper or, depending on the angle, Leatherface from *The Texas Chainsaw Massacre*. He also cuts the shrubs with a machete, wielding it with gladiator-like precision.

I notice everyone here uses a machete, and it is as common to see someone with it strapped to their side as it is to see someone with a Blackberry in the states. I bought milk yesterday and stood in between two men talking with a machete in each of their hands. If this were ShopRite at home, I would have thrown myself up against the automatic doors to escape, conceivably trampling every child and elderly person in my path. But these men were just picking up some groceries after working in the coffee fields, and no one tried to chop me into little pieces.

Carlos is also responsible for getting the hydraulic gate fixed. We were given a remote clicker for it, and when we pressed the button, it creaked open like the gate from *The Adams Family*. We quickly realized the iron gate was too heavy, and the hydraulic system is not strong enough to open it. We drove in, clicked it closed, and it broke five minutes later. So far, it has stayed broken all week. Occasionally, Carlos takes out a pin to the hydraulic on one side so that only half the gate opens. This is supposedly for security reasons so that only a scooter could fit through and not a car. However, Rob and I squeezed our huge rental van through it, so unless the crooks come with an eighteen-wheeler, I am pretty sure they can get in. I also like that a company called Popeye makes the gate. The bread I buy at the market is from a bakery named Popeye. The way things are made here, I am inclined to think they are one and the same company.

There is another way out of the community. This exit is closer to our house but takes you down a very muddy, or dusty depending on the time of the year, road. The road has sharp switchbacks, is not paved, and takes you over the narrow crossing of a busy river. I thought it was a bridge until Rob observed that it is actually a giant metal drum. It allows water to pass through with a blanket of concrete thrown on top, a marvel of engineering ingenuity that was probably designed by the all-encompassing Popeye conglomerate. It is likely one season away from collapsing. That will leave us with only the hydraulic gate exit. I hope that they fix it soon, or Rob and I will have the added charm of driving through a river to get to our house.

In between pretending to get the gate fixed and cutting the grass, Carlos appears very friendly and always likes starting conversations with my husband. Carlos doesn't speak any English, and from what I have observed from their conversations, he couldn't care less that my husband does not understand him. Periodically, Rob tells him he doesn't follow, but Carlos just ignores him and continues with some lengthy story that could involve buying a new tire for his dirt bike or his ideas on a Middle East peace treaty. We will never know. But Rob patiently stands there and listens to him. Many times, Carlos directs the conversation toward Rob's muscles.

"Musculos grande," Carlos says to Rob while he flexes his own. It appears Carlos is trying to impress Rob with his own physique. Rob shows him the dumbbells we brought down with us and the pull-up bar he installed. He is planning on getting back in shape and has already started his routine. I'm thinking that Carlos is lonely. I also notice he makes no comments when I flex my muscles.

Carlos' son, Francisco, also works on the property. He is twenty years old and never smiles. This doesn't bother me or Rob, but the Jehovah's Witness gets offended. The kid seems okay to me, and he doesn't have two names like Jim/Rodger. I would rather get no smiles from someone with one name than lots of smiles from someone with two names. Francisco also rides his dirt bike past our house but doesn't return the same way. There is nowhere to go past our house but into the forest reserve. He must know some short cut or trail, and I imagine him dodging trees and blasting through rivers like an action adventure hero.

After a few days living here, I noticed someone walking five dogs. I'd heard about a woman the other gringos call *The Crazy Dog Lady* because she walks her dogs without a leash, and their barking annoys the other dogs in the neighborhood. She is originally from North Carolina and walks past my house every day at the same time. Her mutts run up to my house and urinate on the house posts, my yoga mat, and anything that has not been urinated on since the last time they were here. One day, I went out to introduce myself, and I quickly realized that my conversations with her always seem to be centered on animals. She told me her name was Dolores and she tries to save as many animals as she can. I don't know if that makes her crazy or a maverick, but I like her and her love of our little four-legged friends.

Yesterday, she came carrying a long wooden stick across her neck and shoulders with a green parrot perched on top. She asked if I wanted the bird or any other dog she owns. Every day, I explain to her I can't: my dog does not get along with others. But she continues to ask again as if we never had the conversation.

She then goes on to tell me she has been robbed seven times. In fact, every story she tells me ends with: then the next day I was robbed. Like, "There were these kids hanging by my house, and I ran over to them and shook my fists and told them to get the hell out of here. Then the next day I was robbed."

Or, "I hired someone to cut my grass, and he wanted thirty dollars. I told him to get the hell out of here, and he is only getting ten. Then the next day I was robbed."

Lastly, my favorite of her tirades was, "My neighbor told me that I was a lunatic, and I told him I'd rather be a lunatic than a raging alcoholic. Then the next day I was robbed."

You get the picture.

I ask her if she changes her routine at all, and say that although I have only known her for a week, I can tell exactly what time she will be passing my house. Dolores says she leaves her car in the driveway so people will think she is home. I try to explain to her that this master security plan is not working and she might want to walk her dogs at different times during the day. She agrees, says I am the smartest person she's ever met, and is going to sue the American Embassy for the break-ins. I wish her good luck, excuse myself, and return to the house.

Between Dolores and the multiple identities of Jim, there will definitely be lots of odd stories to tell my friends back home. I can always hope that the owners of the Barbie Dreamhouse will eventually show up and be less peculiar than my other neighbors, but having built a ten thousand square foot pink stucco house, what are the chances of that?

Buying A Car With Underwear Money

"How are we going to carry all this money out of the bank? We can't just walk out of here with a paper bag full of cash," I question as money is stacked in front of us.

We just withdrew five thousand dollars' worth of colones, the Costa Rican currency, to buy a twelve thousand dollar car. There is a limit to how much cash you can withdraw from this bank in a single day. We now need to go to another one across town and attempt to withdraw the remaining seven thousand dollars to purchase the vehicle. After the teller finishes counting, she lays out two hundred and fifty bills in a single pile. Costa Rica does not have any currency worth more than twenty dollars, thus creating my towering skyscraper of cash. This has brought a considerable amount of unwanted attention from the other customers standing in line.

"Don't worry," Rob leans in and whispers, "I'm going to stick it in my underwear."

"You're kidding me."

"No I'm not kidding you. I'm going into the bathroom to stuff the cash into my underwear, most in the front with some in the back. I'm pretty sure I can get it all in there." Rob reaches across the desk and slides the neatly piled cash into a plastic shopping bag. He then casually walks to the men's bathroom.

I'm embarrassed to confess that this isn't the first time Rob has hidden things in his underwear. Rob is constantly concerned about crime and feels that his drawers are the safest place to hide sensitive documents. On more than one occasion, our cash and credit cards disappeared into the dark recesses of his pants. I always felt sorry when I bought something from a vendor, giving them the cash that had been against Rob's nether regions for the better part of a sunny afternoon. Now Rob wants to take this a step further and do the same with the five grand.

We never thought we would need to spend so much for a used car. They are expensive because the cars are shipped into the country and taxed heavily, a burden passed on to the buyer. This makes the cost double the blue book value listed in the States, but we had no choice and narrowed our selection down to a four-wheel drive SUV. The harrowing drive across Costa Rica influenced us in owning a powerful vehicle to handle the occasional river and steep mountainous inclines, and since the road to our house takes us through a river and up a steep mountainous incline, an SUV appeared to be the best option. We spend a few days looking at different models and decide on a Mitsubishi Montero, mostly because many people drive them here, and we know it must be cheap to get parts.

While shopping, we notice the dealerships have replaced things in the cars that one doesn't usually see replaced. It wasn't uncommon to see gray seats, a white dashboard, beige glove compartment, and a black steering wheel all in the same vehicle. This patchwork reminds me that this would be an excellent way to hide the effects of the waterlogged cars from Hurricane Katrina, and since some of these cars have "floated" on over to Costa Rica, Rob and I are meticulous when inspecting the inside and outside of the vehicles. I trust Rob since he has a lot of experience fixing cars.

When Rob was in high school, he noticed a puke green 1970 Nova that hadn't moved for the street sweepers in months. It accumulated tickets until there was a pile clipped under the windshield wipers. He left a note asking the owner if he wanted to sell the car. The guy showed up and told him it ran, but someone had stolen both the radiator and the battery. Rob had no idea if it would work but knew Novas had a history of being reliable vehicles. Rob talked the owner down to fifty bucks, went to the junkyard, and bought a battery and radiator. He also took a roller and painted the car with two coats of Benjamin Moore's white outdoor oil paint. That part, he said, was to impress the ladies.

Rob made the necessary repairs, and the Nova ran great until his crazy friend Dom (a guy who used motor oil on his head to clean out his hair follicles), got angry with Rob and shot out two tires, both car doors, and something under the hood that caused the heater to remain on indefinitely. The shoot-out occurred while Rob hid behind an oak tree helplessly watching as his car, and the oak tree, got blasted by a hail of bullets. Once Dom went back inside to lather his head with more oil, Rob jumped in his car and wobbled away on two flat tires.

After going back to the same junkyard, he once again fixed the Nova and used it for his budding career as a car service driver. He picked up customers in a car with bullet holes in the doors, a duct taped window, and a heater blasting in the middle of August not to mention, the passenger door was jammed, making them enter through the driver's side and slide across the bench seat. It was this attention to detail that made the car unforgettable, not only to his paying clients, but also to the girls he tried to pick up while cruising down 86th street.

With that in mind, Rob searched for a vehicle he felt would have the same stamina the old Nova displayed years before. We found a red 1998 Mitsubishi Montero with roughly one hundred thousand miles, priced at twelve thousand dollars. Nobody in their right mind would pay that in the States. We brought our interpreter with us and started to negotiate, but this is where being gringos and pulling up in a rental car hampered us getting a good deal. Desperation is the world's worst cologne, and we reeked of it.

Our interpreter was a sweet seventeen-year-old girl formally from California. She moved here with her parents when she was five and is fluent in Spanish. The owner of the dealership was not present, but the salesman called him and gave the phone to our interpreter. With her help, Rob began the negotiations. I was eager to see what kind of deal we would get. Rob's tough Brooklyn-style bargaining had been successful with us never paying sticker price. He would talk down the price of a turkey sandwich if he thought he could get a better deal.

"Tell him I'll give him ten grand," Rob said. Reluctantly, our interpreter relayed the message.

"He said he'll take twelve thousand dollars," she nervously returned.

"What? Tell him I'll give him ten thousand five hundred." These negotiations went back and forth as our translator got upset. She had not planned on being in the middle of a heated discussion, and at seventeen, I doubt she had ever been placed in this position before. I started to feel bad for her when Rob barked, "I won't go over eleven thousand five hundred. Tell him that's it; I won't pay a penny more."

"Hmm... ah... he's not going to like that."

"Just tell him, that's it; I'll walk." Rob confidently leaned back in his chair as our interpreter meekly relayed the message and consequently pulled the phone away from her ear. All of us heard the screaming. She then put her ear back to the phone, listened for another ten seconds, and turned back to Rob.

"He said he'll take twelve thousand dollars." And that's how we ended up paying full price for our car, the first time in Pisani history. Rob's Brooklyn negotiation skills sucked more than finding a DVD boxed set of Steven Seagal movies under the Christmas tree. I actually thought Rob might walk away, but the thought of paying another week for the rental car caused him to fold. It was the end of an intoxicating era.

I was thinking we were finished when the owner requested something out of the ordinary and more than a little suspicious. He wanted the money deposited into his account before he signed over the title. At first, we thought this was translated wrong. But no, he definitely said it. He promised he would provide us the legal paperwork *after* he received the money. Rob had done his homework and knew that this transaction should be performed in front of an attorney at the time of sale. Once we said we wouldn't provide the money without the paperwork, the owner then wanted the money in cash or he would sell the car to someone else. We had no other choice but to figure out how we could acquire such a humongous sum of money in one day. With all the modern fraud protection on bank accounts, we knew this would not be an easy task.

I am now waiting for Rob to return from the bathroom with the five grand in his pants. We took the maximum cash advances on our credit cards and as much money as we could from our checking account. Finally, after several hours, we end up with less than half the money. Rob walks out of the bathroom and we try the same procedure at another bank. Luckily, they allow us to withdraw the remaining seven grand. We now need to walk two blocks with Rob carrying all of the cash in his underpants. Forgive me for being paranoid, but I get a little uncomfortable running all over a Central American town with twelve grand in my husband's tighty-whities.

Rob exits the men's room and waddles toward me with his grossly distorted pelvis. His pants are pulled up to his navel to prevent the money from pulling his underwear down. This gives him an unflattering case of high waters. I am unclear how this will help us blend into the crowd since my husband now looks like Jerry Lewis. We leave the bank and make a run for our car.

"You go first, and I'll follow," Rob says as he waddles across the street. He always makes me go first, another one of his security precautions, but this time it doesn't make much sense since he is the one carrying the money and the one most likely to get hit over the head. Taking one last glance at his mismatched socks, I decide to take his advice and walk as far away from him as possible.

"This is crazy... the whole thing... it's nuts," I say as Rob opens the car door for me. "I feel like everything is harder here. How are we supposed to get anything done if buying a car is so damn difficult?"

"It's just a snag, a small inconvenience. Today we will get the car and return the rental. It's one more thing we can put behind us." Rob starts the car, and we head to the dealership's attorney. He is bilingual, so we will have a modest idea of what the hell he is talking about. It doesn't take long for him to invite us into his office, where he lays out a variety of papers for us to sign. However, the SUV is not here yet. We ask the attorney to call the dealership and find out what the holdup is. When he reaches the owner over the phone, we can overhear him screaming, and the only bit I understand is *crazy gringo*. Just what you want to hear with twelve grand stacked in front of you.

"What's the problem?" Rob asks.

"There seems to be an issue, Senor. He doesn't want to sell it to you anymore."

"Why the hell not?"

"He says you did not trust him. He wanted you to deposit the money into his account, and you didn't, and I don't think he likes gringos too much," the attorney says as he pulls at his buttoned collar. Rob stands up and approaches him.

"If you think I am going to walk out of here with twelve thousand dollars in my pants... well... you're out of your fucking mind. How many other people know I have this money?" Rob's voice gets louder with each step toward the attorney. "I want you to call him back, tell him we did everything he asked, except we want a legal transaction just like any other Tico in Costa Rica. You got that?" They're standing face to face, and I see a bead of sweat trickle down the attorney's forehead.

He quickly grabs his phone, and a salesman drives up with the SUV in less than five minutes.

The paperwork appears to be in order, all but the amount of three thousand dollars he put down as the purchase price, another way the dealership can avoid paying additional taxes, but we don't care. We sign everything, and the salesman hands us the keys and one license plate.

"Where's the other one?" I ask.

"You only need one in Costa Rica," he says before swiftly leaving the office. We walk out to the street and soon notice all the other vehicles have two license plates. I am not surprised; the guy had all the intentions of screwing us one way or the other, but on the bright side, I do get great satisfaction knowing they are handling money that sat in Rob's sweaty underpants.

The most important thing is that we have a car and can return the rental today. And even if they got one past us, at least the car is in my name.

I think.

Pointing North, Falling Boulders, & Biting Ants

"Pura Vida!" Carlos says while Rob rinses soapy water off the car hood. It's not even nine in the morning, and Rob is already eager to show off our new SUV. Without the stress of work, he actually takes pleasure in keeping our vehicle clean, and believe me, he did not show this type of enthusiasm back in the States. His car was so messy he parked it behind his office so patients couldn't glance inside. One evening driving home from work, I pulled next to Rob at a red light and saw him salting two hard-boiled eggs over his lap. When he noticed me watching and shaking my head, he took the shells and tossed them over his shoulder into the back seat. It explained where all my salt shakers disappeared to and why his scrubs always smelled like an egg salad sandwich.

Carlos smiles at me and announces the broken hydraulic gate will be repaired by Friday. This is exactly what he said last week and will likely say a week from now. Ticos don't like to give bad news. They would rather just tell you something good and hope you care as little about the situation as they do. Jim, the Jehovah's Witness, took it upon himself to wrap a chain and padlock around the gate so no one could enter unless they had the key. Under normal circumstances, this would be fine. However, the size of it resembles the shackle used to secure King Kong during his theatrical debut.

It is my job to unlock the gate, open it for Rob to drive through, and wrap the chain back around it. I always volunteer to do this Herculean chore except at night or in the rain. The chain is extremely heavy, and the rusted padlock refuses to close unless I slam the bottom with the palm of my hand. Half my fingers are already black and blue. I tolerate this assignment since the hydraulics will be fixed, as Carlos promises, this Friday for sure.

Rob directs Carlos inside the car and points to all the free bonus items: the prehistoric 1985 cassette player, a broken cigarette lighter, and the digital compass in the dashboard that points north no matter which direction we are headed. But my favorite is the anti-theft AM/FM radio. Turning it on requires one to enter a numeric combination more complex than The Da Vinci Code. I have not yet cracked this riddle, and until I can find my Night Ranger Greatest Hits tape, I don't think I will be using the cassette player, either. It all seems to please Carlos until he notices the car has only one license plate.

"Donde esta?" he asks. We tell him our story, and he shakes his head. Carlos says we need two and urges us to go back and get the other. I would rather squeeze the two-ton chain and padlock around my neck until I lapse into unconsciousness. There is no way I'm going back there.

Rob explains to Carlos we're driving to Arenal Volcano to do a little sightseeing. Carlos smiles, raises his arms in a sweeping gesture, and shouts: **BOOM.** With that, he walks away with a shovel in hand and whistles as he walks back down the mountain. This was, by far, the best way to end a conversation, and I'm seriously considering adopting it as my own departing farewell with friends.

Arenal Volcano is a major tourist attraction, and I can't imagine it would be that dangerous. Now that we have our own car, we want to venture out and see all the beautiful and interesting places in Costa Rica. We check out our map and plan a trip for the following day. I'm excited to witness what others have said is one of the most spectacular displays of volcanic activity. I can hardly sleep thinking about how amazing the next couple days will be.

One hour and two police stops later, we are close to our volcanic destination. We should have listened to Carlos since the missing front license plate has become a major issue. The traffic police position themselves on the side of the road and point at cars to pull over. They keep spotting our missing plate because we are driving straight toward them. Some gringos have advised us to keep driving since the police cannot leave their post. My idea of paradise is not running from the cops in a foreign country, although I have a feeling Rob might take a chance if I wasn't in the car. After the second police stop, Rob grabs a screwdriver and moves the back license plate to the front, thus preventing the cops from noticing. This modification appears to be working; we haven't been harassed since.

As we drive, always north as my trusted dashboard compass advertises, I open my travel book and serenade Rob with all the fun facts I am learning. "Not only will we witness molten boulders tumble down the volcano, if we are lucky, we might see "pyroclastic avalanches". What the hell is that supposed to mean?"

"Not sure... sounds exciting, though... lovin' it... keep reading," Rob replies.

"There was a huge eruption in 1968, and the volcano has remained active for over four hundred years. Are you sure this is safe?"

"Absolutely. What are the odds anything happens while we're there?"

I consider the statistical chances of his last comment. "You're right. It would be pretty awesome watching molten boulders sliding down a volcano. How many times does someone get to witness that?"

"Hopefully more than once," Rob mumbles under his breath. I glance to another chapter and read about the wildlife around the volcano. It has both a primary and secondary tropical forest, hundreds of species of birds, and lots and lots of bugs. That doesn't surprise me. After my thorough investigation about Costa Rica, I know it can be buggy here. I read further as the author describes being bit by a bullet ant.

A bullet ant is approximately an inch long and has a sting that makes one feel as if shot with a bullet. It's a burning/ throbbing pain that lasts twenty-four hours. Some tribes around the world use this as an initiation rite for a boy to become a warrior. The boy wears an ant-filled glove for ten minutes, resulting in his arm becoming paralyzed for twenty-four hours, but don't congratulate the young man just yet; he has to do this twenty times before he can graduate to warrior.

Wow, that sounds like the crappiest Bar Mitzvah ever. I relay the story to Rob, who says he would immediately start a new tribe, absolutely refusing to participate in such hijinks. I love that about my husband; he's a real go-getter, impenetrable to peer pressure, a man who would pack his spear, move away from his idiotic glove-wearing friends, and find a new neighborhood where his tribe is more concerned with making good pizza. Rob has a long history of complaining about any pizza not made in Brooklyn. It hasn't helped that every slice we've eaten so far in Costa Rica tasted like a taco. This causes Rob to lecture for thirty minutes about the merits of fresh mozzarella to anyone listening. Unfortunately, the only person listening is me.

I tell Rob about the author's bullet ant experience, "He's walking through the forest wearing shorts, and a bullet ant bites right into his leg. What a knucklehead."

"Didn't *you* wear capri pants when we hiked up that mountain? And didn't *you* wear shorts when we rode a horse? Don't be so hard on the guy," Rob scolds.

"I wore shorts that day because I was unaware I would be getting my first horseback riding lesson, remember? You sort of left that part out."

We see a mountain in the distance with clouds hovering over the top quarter. It must be the volcano, but it doesn't look as ominous as I imagined. Tourists are biking in the streets, walking along the sidewalks, and no one looks terrified that an active volcano is looming over their heads. We see a sign for our hotel and turn down an unpaved, bumpy road. This gives us a chance to feel how good the shocks work. It doesn't take long to learn they suck pretty bad. The shocks are nowhere near as dependable as the more expensive SUV we rented when we first drove across Costa Rica.

"Maybe we can get them replaced," Rob suggests. It depresses me almost as much as my cassette player.

With my brain scrambled from the bumpy ride, we check into the hotel and begin unpacking. I search for my sensible cargo pants, but they are not in my bag; they are inconveniently hanging back home in the closet. I change into a pair of capris, walk over to the window, and pull the curtains open. We have a direct and *very* close view of the volcano.

"Wow, do you think it's safe to be here?" I don't wait for a response as I find the evacuation plan on the back of the closet door. "Okay, so if this thing blows, we run to a farm on the south side and wait for a helicopter to rescue us. Good to know." Rob walks out onto a balcony that's perfect for watching the volcano. Since it is already late, we get dinner and hang out in the room for the rest of the evening.

We wait and wait but don't see a thing. The volcano is hiding in a cloud of dense fog, obscuring any view. This really stinks. If I had my computer, I would type a review to TripAdvisor.com and tell them this was a big waste of time. The wealthy people who usually post negative reviews would have a field day with this. How can this be one of Costa Rica's biggest attractions when there is nothing to see? It's worse than a booger on a bedpost.

We turn in, hoping the next day will be more exciting than the first. Around three in the morning, we wake to a loud explosion that jolts us out of bed. The lights fade in and out like Frankenstein's laboratory.

Rob looks out the window and witnesses an unconstrained propulsion of boulders. I start to panic, look at the evacuation route, and contemplate whether wrapping myself in the polyester orange curtains will get me noticed by a passing helicopter. I decide against it, fearing the polyester-blend is flammable and escaping a volcano might go smoother without cloaking myself in combustible fabrics. Before I run screaming into the night, I go outside, where Rob is standing on the balcony. Cameras are flashing from other terraces; ooh's and aah's echo in the darkness.

"Is this normal?" Rob yells out to the group of photographers in the distance.

We hear a man yell back.

"Sure is! This is a lucky night, but it won't last long."

Rob runs to get his camera and starts snapping pictures as fast as he can. Large, molten rocks propel out the cone of the volcano and tumble down its side. These rocks are the size of eighteen-wheelers and look as if they are thundering toward the hotel. They glow brightly, leaving a trail of fiery stones in their wakes. This is all happening several miles away, and although I am nervous, I've never seen anything more fabulous in my life. The steady currents of blazing rocks make for a dazzling show that I will never forget, and just like the man said, the production slows down until only a trickle of boulders shoot out from the top.

"I think we just saw a pyroclastic avalanche," Rob says.

I now understand why Carlos yelled **BOOM** after we told him we were coming here. He was just preparing us for what was in store. I like the guy even more now.

The next day, we prepare for our hike; Rob wears his long jeans while I wear my capris. He glances at my clothes but doesn't make a comment. He knows if I packed the right pants, I would be wearing them now. We follow signs to a trail and walk into the thick forest. The canopy of trees darkens our route as we go deeper into the brush. The primary forest has an extra effect of eeriness. It gives you a glimpse of what the earth looked like before humans existed, and it awakens a long buried primordial instinct, a feeling that you can't explain but still skates along your genetic code.

As we walk along the trail, we hear something rustle in the forest. We stop walking and see a three foot bird hop onto the trail. He continues walking ahead of us, periodically looking back. He doesn't seem scared, so we follow him as if he's our personal tour guide. This will make a great picture, so I stop, lean on a tree, and reach for my camera. I am about to snap a photo when I feel a piercing pain. I look down and see a bullet ant biting my exposed ankle.

"I'VE BEEN HIT," are my last words before collapsing into a trail of harmless leaf cutter ants. My avian tour guide has betrayed me. The bird takes one look at my quivering corpse and runs back into the forest. I hold onto my ankle and lay in the dirt as the leaf cutter ants march single file over my body carrying miniscule leaves on their backs while trying to make it back to their nest. The big, screaming imbecile in their way doesn't appear to slow them down one bit.

"Are you okay, Sweetie? Talk to me. Can you stand?" Rob says as he lifts me to my feet.

"It hurts so friggin bad, I can't believe it, and all I did was lean on a tree. I don't think I can walk on it." Before I have a chance to resist, he sweeps me up in his arms and starts running uphill. "Rob, are you crazy? You don't have to run. You'll give yourself a heart attack."

"I can do it," he says between labored breaths. Rob leaps over fallen logs and across tree stumps, all while holding me tight against his chest. He's the Bruce Jenner of Rainforest Olympics, hurdling every obstacle that comes his way while sprinting up the trail. Suddenly he slows down, grunting with each step.

"Are you okay?" I say.

"Shit...I think I just dislocated my hip."

"Let me down; I'll walk. You're going to screw up your hip even more if you keep carrying me."

"If I put you down, how will I know I can save you in a true emergency?"

"That is so stupid. How often are you going to have to save me in a forest? For God's sake, let go of me."

"No way, I'm going to finish this." Rob continues hobbling with me in his arms, grunting with each painful step.

We make it back to the road, and Rob finally lets me down. I walk dragging my leg while Rob limps on his bad hip. We take turns leaning on each other as we stumble down the road like two zombies. Along the way, we meet a honeymoon couple planning to take the same hike. After one look at us, the wife says she isn't going. She turns around and leaves her befuddled husband alone at the entrance to the path. I give a great deal of consideration to this pair and can only imagine that her dream honeymoon was probably at Sandals in the Bahamas, a place where she could enjoy beach volleyball, swim-up bars, and banana-kiwi facials. Instead, she listened to her eco-friendly husband (probably her college boyfriend) and ended up sleeping in a tent and composting her own toilet paper. I give 'em a year.

We lumber our way back to the hotel room and collapse on the bed. The throbbing starts settling into my leg as I look forward to a day of possible numbness and convulsions. Rob limps to the hotel restaurant to get ice for his hip. Although things didn't go exactly as planned, I did get to see a pyroclastic avalanche, all without a mass evacuation and helicopter getaway.

Saving Dolores' Bird

Dolores, the Dog Lady, visits me rain or shine, every morning. Today, she shows up with her five dogs and the same parrot perched on a ten-foot stick. The dogs run ahead of her, and before she makes it to my house, they've already peed on my greenhouse, workout equipment, and anything in between that smells like it's in need of a fresh coat of urine. When one dog is finished, another one stands behind to mark the area that was previously marinated. This continues in what looks like a rehearsed circus performance, each dog knowing its place in line and waiting for its turn to spray my petunias. Beowulf is the head honcho, a yellow Labrador and German Shepard mix that gets first dibs in the cycle. I deal with this spectacle because I feel bad that Dolores is lonely and because my little dog Clementine has a crush on Beowulf.

These visits are usually similar in nature: dogs pee, Clementine chases after Beowulf, and Dolores talks my ear off, but today she asks me if she can go to the bathroom. I point to the house and tell her the bathroom is the first door to the left.

"No," she says. "I'd rather go to the bathroom outdoors so I can be closer to nature."

I then see her walk to the side of my house and drop her drawers behind some ornamental grasses. After she is done, she walks back to the front of the house and continues her previous conversation as if her bathroom episode never occurred. Not only do I have to tolerate her dogs urinating all over my house, I now have to endure Dolores whizzing all over my property, too.

I'm actually glad she is here because I want to ask her about getting a driver's license. My United States license is valid, but eventually I will need to get a new one in this country. I don't know where to go and hope that Dolores can fill me in on the details. It's unnerving that I am going to their Department of Motor Vehicles without knowing the language. It's not a fun process in the United States, so I can't imagine it will be better here. Rob doesn't appear concerned and thinks that someone there will be able to help us out. So far, things are going well, and we even accomplished buying a car. After that experience, I feel like nothing else can be that bad. Moving has forced me to get out of my comfort zone, and with each small triumph, I feel like I am planting deeper roots here. Motor Vehicles is just another test to challenge me. However, when I try mentioning this to Dolores, she tells me she never got her license and suggests only an idiot would bother trying.

This is not unlike our morning discussions. These conversations usually center on Dolores' inability to have normal conversations. She complains about living in Costa Rica, complains about her car, and complains that every friend of hers complains too much. It's the type of conversation where I don't need to say a word. You could walk away, read the first volume of the Encyclopedia Britannica, come back outside, and she would still be in the middle of her conspiracy theory that someone is spiking her cappuccino with Windex. On the list of the many ways in which to acquire diarrhea in Costa Rica, I never anticipated the verbal kind I am subjected to everyday from Dolores.

After a couple hours and a few bathroom trips into my bushes, Dolores takes off and leaves me to enjoy my mountain and wash down my yoga mat. Surprisingly, these are the moments I look forward to most. A good dose of Dolores is enough to make you appreciate the moments without her. An hour later, she calls to say her parrot flew off the stick and is now sitting in a tree in front of the Barbie Dreamhouse. I hold my hand over the receiver and ask Rob if he thinks he can get the bird. He rolls his eyes, and I tell Dolores we will meet her in fifteen minutes.

"How does she think I'm going to catch the bird?" Rob asks.

"I didn't know what to say; she was crying, and that poor bird is going to die. She's not native to this area; I can't imagine she will last long out here stuck in a tree."

We walk down the mountain and meet Dolores. The bird has flown onto a tree branch that hangs above the security wall in front of the Barbie Dreamhouse. Rob asks her how the parrot got so high.

"Duh, she flew," Dolores says.

"I thought you clipped her wings."

"I clipped her wings a year ago. It's a miracle she can fly again." Apparently, Dolores does not realize that bird wings need to be clipped regularly or the feathers grow back. Instead of Rob returning her charming "duh" reply, he bites his tongue, smiles at her, then turns to me with that annoyed why-the-hell-did-you-volunteer-me look. It was not bad enough for Rob to see this lady take a leak under his bedroom window, now he has to rescue her bird.

The front security wall is made of volcanic rock stacked at least ten feet high. There is no mortar between the rocks, and if you try to climb the wall, the stones crumble beneath your feet. Rob walks around the house, climbs up a chain link fence, and jumps atop the volcanic wall. Like a performer in the Flying Wallendas, he starts walking it like a tight rope, arms outstretched, taking one step at a time while rocks slip from under his feet. I can clearly see he is apprehensive, which makes me feel awful that I talked him into doing this. He begins to sweat as each step dislodges more rock.

He slowly slides to the tree and looks up. The bird is sitting on a branch many feet away. Dolores hands the ten foot stick over to him, and Rob reaches out, leans toward the tree, and stretches it to the bird. Dolores is yelling out instructions in Spanish, either to Rob or the bird, I don't know which. The bird isn't budging, and Rob starts to worry out loud that he does not have health insurance and is now standing on top a volcanic wall that is crumbling beneath his feet. The image of him in a full body cast does not appear to faze Dolores, but instead, she continues bossing Rob around, urging him to stand on his tiptoes to reach the bird.

While on his toes, Rob tries to push the stick under the bird's legs. At the same time, Dolores shrieks, "SHE DOESN'T LIKE THAT!" He tries again, but the bird ignores the prod and steps back. "STAND STILL," she yells. He remains frozen, one arm holding a ten foot pole straight in the air and one leg off the ground to balance his weight. He looks precisely like Mary Poppins before liftoff.

The bird does not move, so Dolores suggests we should sing to her, together, like in a musical theater production. Dolores starts first, and then Rob and I follow. We sing in unison "la la loo...la la...bonita bird..." like a bunch of criminally insane people. I am hoping the people who live in this house are not home because surely they will shoot each one of us off their property, or at the very least, I will not be able to stick my head in between the wrought iron gates every morning and stare into their front yard.

After five minutes of singing, the bird has mercy on us and walks onto the end of the stick. The parrot, like Rob on the wall, walks the stick one step at a time, balancing herself until she is firmly in the middle. He then hands the stick back down to Dolores. She reprimands the bird for doing something as unthinkable as attempting to fly to freedom, an escape, without a doubt, the parrot has been strategically planning since day one. Dolores then goes into a long and incoherent rant about how no one here likes her or would ever help her. With that, she turns and walks away without thanking us. I can hear her singing to the bird as she walks into the forest, a forest with a lot of tall trees.

Rob and I go home and take the phone off the hook. I promise Rob I will never volunteer him again for anything "Dolores" related, but befriending Dolores reminds me of the cloud forest. There is no way to escape it. The clouds crawl under doors, sneak through windows, and eventually hijack the house, and I am confident avoiding Dolores will prove just as tricky.

Going Postal and Motor Vehicles

There is one compelling reason to get a Costa Rica driver's license: the ability to get cheaper admissions to parks and attractions. For example, the tourist price to see Poas Volcano is seven dollars per person, versus only a little over a dollar for Ticos. You actually need to show your residency card, but other gringos say their Costa Rica driver's license works just as well. It would be a considerable savings, so I agree to go to Motor Vehicles, a place with little promise of a positive experience.

I grew up only ten minutes away from the New Jersey Department of Motor Vehicles. The building sits next door to Rahway State Prison, a name later changed to East Jersey State Prison as requested by the citizens of Rahway. Apparently, many residents felt that having a maximum security prison named after their city decreased property values. I would argue that it was living near a maximum security prison that decreased property values, but what do I know about the economics of real estate? Regardless, changing the name of it made the fastidious villagers happy, and they all rejoiced in their cul-de-sacs.

I always thought the community should have embraced their semi-famous clinker. Movies are always shot there, and the prison has the distinction of being the facility where the 1978 Academy Award winning documentary *Scared Straight* was filmed. This is a small piece of trivia my father is strangely proud of. He found this a perfectly acceptable way to prevent juvenile delinquents from re-offending and would threaten my sister and me with this program if we continued smacking each other in the back seat. Since Motor Vehicles was next to the prison, I got to relive this endearing childhood memory every time I renewed my driver's license.

At first, I didn't want a Costa Rican license, thinking it was a great way to avoid paying a ticket. Where would they mail it if we were not in the system? Nevertheless, mail doesn't seem to be an issue because we don't get any. None. Unlike the American structure of mail service and basic common sense, there are no house numbers or street signs anywhere. I recently found out my actual address is something like "six hundred meters south of the mango tree." I now have to listen to my dad argue with me that I am hiding my real address from him, for no other reason than I want to hide my real address from him. All this confirms the sneaky suspicion my dad already has about me; I left the States for some nefarious reason. It couldn't be that I just hated my job, something everyone on this side of the hemisphere already knows.

After a couple weeks, I realize that getting no mail has greatly decreased my anxiety levels. I like not having a box full of credit card applications, circulars, and catalogs that keep coming even though my last purchase from that store was in 1995. It's less clutter, not only in my house, but in my brain. The whole point of moving here was to simplify my life, and that's impossible if you are saturated every waking second with advertisements, and although Domino's new cheesy crust pizza sounds delicious, I don't need to read about it every day. However, it would explain why I ate the new cheesy crust pizza three nights a week.

It's great that you do not need to get mail to pay your bills. Their system is easy: while at the supermarket, you can pay for your electric and phone bills along with your groceries. The arrangement is surprisingly uncomplicated. Somehow, in the States we have a way of making some of the simplest things more difficult, exponentially making life harder and less fulfilling. Living here is teaching me to trim off the excess to make room for what makes me most content, and clearly, that excess includes a lot of junk mail.

Technically, there is a mail carrier gallivanting around. I frequently compare him to a folklore creature, like Sasquatch or The Loch Ness Monster: often talked about but rarely seen. I did catch a sighting of him as I drove down the mountain one morning. He was leaning against his scooter with a small messenger bag strapped across his chest. He didn't appear hurried, considering he was in the same place when I drove back up the mountain an hour later. He spent sixty minutes of his workday talking with a beautiful woman who appeared delighted to share his company. The man was the happiest postal worker I've ever seen, and why wouldn't he be? All in all, it looks like a great job. "Going Postal" probably has a completely different meaning here than in the States. It would not be synonymous with workplace rage, but with something as cheerful as eating dessert or climbing a tree. I can imagine the kids on the playground scream, "Let's go postal!" before merrily running to an ice cream truck. There are really great reasons to live here. I hope that going to Motor Vehicles is one of them.

Just as we are about to exit Valley Ranch, we see Dolores and her dogs walk toward our car. We give her a short greeting and tell her we are on our way to get our licenses.

"HAH, you're both crazy. Hope you get it, but you need a medical exam first. You know that, right... AN EXAM WITH A DOCTOR," she barks. Her eyes protrude out of her head like someone who just heard raccoons are taking over the city and establishing a new rule of law.

"A what? I have to see a doctor before getting my license?" I ask.

"Yup, you sure do. They have a bunch of medical offices outside Motor Vehicles. Go to one of those shit holes. That's what the other gringos do. They are all a bunch of shit holes."

I'm not sure if the last "shit hole" comment was concerning the gringos or the medical offices, but I don't ask her to clarify, worried her eyeballs might pop completely out of her head. We drive off with the troubling information that we have to go to a medical office first. I hop out of the car to open the behemoth padlock on the gate, possibly for the last time since the hydraulics will be fixed, as Carlos promised, next Friday for sure.

The whole medical thing sounds scammy. A bunch of doctor offices around Motor Vehicles? The only thing I know about this process is I have to pay for something at the bank first. I don't know what it is, but Rob doesn't seem bothered by this. As a perpetual organizer, my brain cannot work this way. I must know all the details, unlike Rob, who says, "Hey, how bad can it be? We will figure it out when we get there." This might be okay if we spoke the language; however, Rob does not consider this an obstacle. His method works most of the time, and due to default, my life has taken on this quirky solution to all my Costa Rican predicaments.

As I previously mentioned, there are no street signs in Costa Rica. It is impossible to get directions from anyone, so we spend the majority of our time just finding a place, sometimes to come back the next day to do what we had intended to do the day before. But we get lucky this time and find the location, only because a guy is standing in the street with a dirty, ripped cardboard sign that reads *Medical Exam*, a sign I would more likely expect to see on the side of a dirt road at a refugee camp. We find a parking space and ask the kid with the sign where to go.

Donde esta doctor? Por favor?

The kid points to a garage.

It looks like a place where, at the very least, we can place a bet on dog fighting... buy a kilo of coke... or plan a hit on your spouse. We stand there confused and unsure what to do. However, after seeing people walk in, and with no better option, we decide to follow the crowd.

We enter a dirty waiting room with plastic chairs and a man behind a counter asking us for ten thousand colones each (approximately twenty dollars). In return, he gives us a small piece of paper and points to the chairs. Across from us is a standing, decapitated female mannequin wearing a pair of soiled corduroy shorts. The room looks like the opening scene of a horror flick. Wasn't Hannibal Lector a doctor?

My mind races, and I am sure I hear screaming victims in the back room trying to claw their way out of a twenty foot hole. My heart starts to pound, and I look next to me at a woman casually reading a romance novel. Nobody would read a book with Fabio on the cover if she were in mortal danger, so I calm down and take in my surroundings. I start to think about all the attention I placed on my waiting room when I was a chiropractor: beautiful wallpaper, scented candles, and relaxing music. Would my patients appreciate the dirty chairs and the stained walls, not to mention, *The Silence of the Lambs* theme? Not surprisingly, there is no suggestion box to voice my concerns.

I go into the untidy exam room first and answer a variety of questions regarding my health. Thankfully, the doctor speaks English. He is in his early thirties and presents himself with all the authority of someone who wants me out of here as quick as possible, a position I find myself in more times than I'd like to admit. I take no offense as I quickly read an eye chart, get weighed and measured like a steer up for auction, and finally walk out with a stamped piece of paper with the instructions to bring in the next patron. It probably took no longer than seven minutes. As Rob goes in, I start talking to an American couple who tell me I need residency to get a license. Rob and I have not even begun getting all the paperwork needed to apply for permanent residency in Costa Rica, and I never considered I needed it to get a license.

"You need to be in the system," they say, "but, like anything else in Costa Rica, that might not be the case today."

This totally ticks me off; we just blew forty dollars for a ridiculous medical exam and might not even get a license. I tell this to Rob after his exam, and as always, he is calm and says we should at least try since we are here.

We go to the bank and pay the fee for something that I am unsure has anything to do with getting our license. We take that receipt, walk next door to Motor Vehicles, and stand in line to get the copies of our passports stamped. Costa Rica is all about stamps, and I am inclined to get a bunch of generic ones and stamp the hell out of my documents. I really don't think they would know the difference. Now the rest of the story is surprisingly similar to America: lines, then another line, and then another. We sit in chairs, and as the next person is helped, we each have to move down a seat. The room looks like we are doing the wave at a sporting event: up, down, up down. We have no idea what each line is for; we just go through the motions. Nobody here speaks English, and all I can keep saying is that Costa Rica is beautiful, *Muy bonita Costa Rica,* in some Tourette-like, *Rain Man* sort of way. Some look irritated with me, and some feel downright sorry for me. I feel sorry for myself right about now.

Finally, we are the next people in the last line, and we get our licenses. "Gracias, mucho rapido, muy bonita Costa Rica," I exclaim in jubilation. I don't think I would have done this without Rob. No, I definitely wouldn't have even tried. With each hurdle I cross, I begin to feel more optimistic. This strange road I walk, one leg physically in Costa Rica and one mentally in America, is slowly becoming easier. Instead of a bumpy, jolting ride, the road is becoming a bit smoother.

In the end, I don't know if we actually needed to be residents, or if maybe it was our lucky day. It took a mere five hours, and Rob confidently announces, "I knew we could do it. It really wasn't that bad, was it?" To answer that question, all you need to see is the picture on my license. I look as if I am trying to claw out of a twenty foot hole.

Farmers' Market

Most every town in Costa Rica has a farmers' market with hundreds of stalls showcasing a wide range of produce. It's so awesome that I wish I could have shopped like this years ago. Back then, my shopping experience consisted of darting through the store and filling my cart with processed food. Like many other working couples, we never had time to cook, so I rarely bought fresh fruits or vegetables. If it was in a box and microwavable, it found a home in my freezer. I have genetically modified my DNA; ten years eating a diet high in trans-fat can do that to you. It left me bloated and moody most of the time, just the right amount of emotional instability to make Rob hide from me every time I came home from work.

When I finally felt it was time to detox my battered liver, I bought fruit but never considered the environmental impact of how far the food had to travel to my plate. I was so wrapped up in my daily routine, I never gave a free thought as to how our government was regulating our food industry. Nevertheless, I do consider myself a thoughtful consumer when it comes to the ethical treatment of animals. Veal consumption ended at nine years old after watching a sickening documentary about the treatment of calves. I also stopped eating lamb once I figured out lamb came from, well, a lamb. And just to round things out, I don't wear fur or eat peas. I have equally strong aversions to both.

My goal is to change my bad habits and adopt a Costa Rican diet. I want to be the type of person who will eat a piece of fruit instead of an Oreo, the hostess who proudly offers carrots and celery sticks to her guests instead of cheese puffs. I'd also like to have a regular bowel movement, the kind that rings in the morning like a New Orleans Dixieland band. My goals have become considerably shorter since quitting my job.

Rob and I both start our healthy makeover and look forward to the farmers' market. We get there early for a better chance at picking the ripest fruits and vegetables. The vendors are constantly spraying their produce with water and calling out to the crowds to come inspect their assortment. There is a lot of competition here; farmers line up with similar items next to each other so a beautiful display will surely grab your attention away from another competitor. I've never seen anything like this before, a kaleidoscopic show with the most colorful, juiciest produce that's available. Shoppers bring their own folding shopping carts; it's the easiest way to wind around the narrow aisles. Some people don't bother buying one but will use a tall laundry basket with casters attached to the bottom. Why blow twenty bucks on a cart when you can get double use out of your clothes basket?

Something else happens here that is noticeably different than in the States: everyone is friendly, often holding their new bouquet of fresh flowers while calling *Pura Vida* to their colleagues and friends. Groups of people stop in the middle of the aisle, and no one shouts at them to get out of the way. It's a social gathering as much as a shopping experience. There is a real sense of community with a value placed on the connections people have with each other. Some of the retired gringos say it reminds them of the 1950's. I appreciate the chance to know what that feels like, to experience life at a slower pace, when buying fresh bread is the perfect opportunity to greet your neighbor with a friendly hello. If there is a better way to live, I've certainly found it here.

After a couple months of shopping at the market, we picked our favorite vendors. We repeat our business with them every Saturday. The pineapple man is a boisterous fifty year old with a handlebar mustache. He calls out to the crowd with an auctioneer's voice, giving out samples of his fruit. His pineapples taste like Jolly Ranchers; they are so sweet and succulent, I enjoy eating them for dessert. He must pick them at the ripest times, possibly the day before the market. Either that or he personally injects each one with fructose. I don't see any syringes lying around, so I will assume it's just the fermenting sugar.

"Two pineapples for five hundred colones," he calls out. Five hundred colones is approximately ninety cents, a huge bargain for two pineapples. The last time I checked in the States, a pineapple was four dollars. It is a striking difference in the cost of living between the two countries.

I feel like I'm in the middle of a food renaissance, tasting and eating produce we never knew existed. It's a long way from my days roaming down a frozen food aisle and tossing a week's worth of Hot Pockets in my cart. One afternoon in Costco, I bought a gigantic box of Pop Tarts and one hundred single packaged cream cheese bags. I thought the individually packaged cream cheese wouldn't spoil as quickly. Rob looked at the date and realized we only had six weeks before it expired. Twice a day, every day, Rob ate a Pop Tart with a spread of cream cheese. Twenty pounds later, he made me swear never to buy anything in bulk again. Now we don't buy anything frozen and rarely anything that is prepackaged. Living here is the best place to lose weight and get healthy, something mirrored by all the thin Costa Ricans walking around.

Not far from the pineapple stand is my tomato lady, a middle-aged woman who works the stall with her elderly father. Her tomatoes are fat, red, and—unlike in Italy—you can pick them up and fondle them unmercifully. I've never before had the temptation to eat a tomato like an apple, but these are so good I can't wait to take a bite.

She reaches down under the stall and brings up a bag of her best tomatoes, which she put aside for us. I am touched. She is careful as she weighs them, making sure we see the numbers registering how much each cost. Currently, a kilo of tomatoes cost $1.27. Since a kilo is 2.2 pounds, the cost for a pound of tomatoes is fifty-seven cents. At these prices, we eat a lot of tomatoes. We put them on sandwiches, in salads, and sometimes hollow them out and fill them with tuna fish.

I'm starting to enjoy living in a place where even my interaction with the tomato lady is pleasurable. So often, we are in such a rush we forget to show even the smallest amount of kindness to those around us, but when you value the present moment, you don't get lost with plans of the future or thoughts of what happened in the past. Buddhism calls this having "a monkey mind," a brain that cannot focus on what's actually right before you but sends you into a whirlpool of anxiety and obsessive thoughts. It's funny that I have less of a monkey mind in a country that actually has monkeys.

Our garlic vendor waves at me through the crowd. She's a beautiful woman who flashes a bright smile as she shows us the current price for her garlic, one of the few things at the market that is imported. All the heads of garlic are in little mesh casings from China. She also has locally grown garlic, but that is more expensive and always looks small and ruddy in comparison to the ones from China. We always buy the garlic from China, but today we decide to buy the funny looking local kind. It smells just as good, and I am sure tastes the same. This is another lesson learned after leaving the States. I was used to eating perfect, waxy fruit without any scars or blemishes thanks to those nice people at the pesticide companies.

While I practice my Spanish with the garlic lady, Rob wanders off to buy cabbage. The man selling it looks exactly how you would expect a cabbage farmer to look. He is burly, plump, and as round as his cabbage. This is definitely the kind of guy you want on your side during a bar brawl. He greets my husband like a long lost brother, shaking Rob's hand with the strength of a guy who is strong enough to haul a ton of cabbage heads. Although Rob can't understand him, the cabbage guy talks rapidly about what I assume is all the work that went into today's harvest. His cabbage is the size of a pumpkin and only costs twenty-seven cents. It lasts the entire week. We use it as a topping for our bean burritos or in a chicken stir-fry dish. It's a great way to thicken a meal and make the servings last for a week. I might have found the first secret to living fantastically on our drastically reduced budget: a diet full of cabbage.

We walk over to the young pepper farmer. He is a teenager who works the stand every week for his family. He picks out the best peppers and puts them on top of the pile. The boy has beautiful skin with traces of youthful rosiness in his cheeks. He's busy wrestling his curly hair into a baseball cap while watching us fill our plastic bag. Each pepper costs eighteen cents.

The rest of the morning, we continue stopping at our favorite vendors. We snatch up celery for twenty cents, a kilogram of green beans for one dollar, and a loaf of Italian bread for seventy cents. While I wait for a bag of freshly ground coffee, Rob walks over to the egg stand. Now that Rob is starting his bodybuilder diet, he is eating five egg whites a day. The egg farmer is thrilled when he sees my husband coming. He must think Rob is about to drop dead from cholesterol. Until that happens, he is happy to sell him four dozen eggs each week. Each egg costs roughly twenty cents.

Overall, the cost for a week of fruits and vegetables comes to twenty dollars. If you throw in some chicken, it's closer to twenty-six dollars. I used to spend this much ordering Chinese food after one night of work. I wasted so much money eating out, especially on food that was making me fat and crabby. Since I began introducing a healthier diet, the thin veil of depression that has followed me around for years has disappeared. I appreciate that Costa Rica makes it possible for their citizens to afford healthy food. It seems ridiculous that the United States does not follow this logic. We tend to do precisely the opposite.

The corn industry is subsidized in America. A major product created is high fructose corn syrup, a sugar substitute used in soft drinks, cereals, and many other foods. It is cheaper than sugar and is widely viewed as one of the reasons obesity levels have skyrocketed. It's a shame the government would rather pay farmers to grow a crop that is increasingly making us sicker instead of subsidizing healthy produce. Why would anyone pay four dollars for a pineapple when they can buy an entire box of cereal bars for two dollars? Making it more affordable would give people a good reason to eat a healthier diet.

Costa Rica has a lot to offer, although I can do without the sporadic electricity, potholes, and Dolores the dog lady. On the flip side, where in the States can I spend twenty-six dollars and eat for a week? Where can I go where someone puts aside the best tomatoes for me? All Americans should have the opportunity to experience this in their own town. There is no doubt our communities would grow stronger if we all interacted with each other. Moreover, if our government gave incentives for farmers to grow more produce, a family of four could eat healthy meals for under fifty dollars a week. It's not such a bad idea, certainly pura vida, if you ask me.

Stop… Or My Husband Will Shoot

One morning in July 1979, my family awoke to a small hole in our living room window. After careful investigation, it proved some little shitter shot a BB gun at our house. This caused considerable alarm and phone calls urgently placed to the authorities. These were the days before CSI, so no fingerprinting was performed or DNA swabs sent to headquarters, but three squad cars did appear and took down the report, shaking their heads in unison concerning the blatant disregard for my mother's picture window and Hummel figurines. The perpetrator was never found, and it was my first encounter with the dark side of living in suburbia.

Rob, on the other hand, wrestled a gun away from a druggie while driving car service. The older drivers would not take the call from the individual bearing a swastika tattoo (handsomely inked on his forehead no less) who staggered into the dispatcher's office. Rob needed the money, took the fare, and ended up fighting for his life. Police were radioed and shook their heads in unison concerning the blatant disregard for calling them while on their coffee break. Needless to say,

Rob has dealt with more than a BB gun in his life, and these experiences have contributed to his impression that people, if given the opportunity, might stick a gun in your face.

Due to these circumstances, Rob searches the Internet for any information about crime in Costa Rica. He's learned that if your car is stolen, it will most likely be held for ransom. The crooks ask for a few hundred dollars, meet you in a park for the exchange, and give you back your car. If I had to choose which crime to be a victim of, this one might be it; I like the non-violent nature. I get to spend an afternoon in the park and can go back to my life without suffering the irksome side effects of Stockholm Syndrome, not a bad day. My sister would probably volunteer her minivan if it guaranteed her a few hours out of the house and away from her three kids.

To prevent this from happening to our car, Rob installed four hidden kill switches: two to disconnect the electricity, another for the fuel pump, and one to directly cut off all power to the battery. He also attached an anti-theft Club to the steering wheel, giving a criminal a well-deserved smack in the nuts if he attempts to turn the car during a getaway. It takes ten minutes to shut off all the kill switches and remove the Club, which confirms that we will never make a quick escape if the need arises. Rob claims his preoccupation with thwarting crime is a result of being married to me.

"You are a liability, but in a good way," Rob comments. "I love you too much to risk anything happening to you."

"I have a hard time believing I am any more of a liability than having you around."

Rob lets out a snort. "Trust me. Having you here makes me extra cautious, and you can't rely on the cops to come, so we need to take care of ourselves. And, don't kid yourself. You're the only person I know who asks crackheads for directions when we get lost." Just for the record, crackheads are better than a GPS. They are more familiar with the neighborhood and know all the back alley short cuts.

After safeguarding the car, Rob decides to thug-proof our house, even though we live on top of a mountain, in a gated community, on a practically inaccessible road. The first thing he does is install battery-operated alarms around the house. A beam emits, and if something passes in front, it will beep a specific number. The back terrace alarm beeps four times; the porch beeps three times, etc. In the event one is activated, we will know exactly where someone is lurking. These alarms are not only sensitive to people, but also to spiders, butterflies, and absolutely nothing at all.

Last night, I awoke to four beeps. Realizing our perimeter had been breached, I peeked through the curtains to discover a black and white calico cat urinating in my basil planter. Rambo Rob never woke up and was totally unaware of the evildoer that invaded our turf. I went back to bed aggravated, more so because I'd been using that basil in my homemade tomato sauce.

In addition to the alarms, Rob buys a machete. He loves his new toy and insists on practicing his swing on a banana tree. One loud crash later, he learns that the trunk of a banana tree is as flimsy as a cardboard toilet paper tube. It will take nine months for the tree to grow back, but worse for Rob, it will be nine months of hearing me lecture about the consequences of swinging a machete around like Babe Ruth at batting practice. Also, he hid the machete tip-down behind our headboard in our bedroom. Since then, it has already fallen over twice: once snipping the phone line in half, and another time narrowly missing my cat's tail. It appears the principal danger of living in Costa Rica is the danger from living with my husband. And, just in case this arsenal is not enough, Rob has just informed me he is going to buy a gun.

"Seriously Rob, why a gun? We have alarms, a machete... why do we need that?"

"Because if I had a gun right now and someone wanted to break in, I'd shoot the bastard." As always, I can rely on Rob to provide interesting dinner conversations.

It's not that I don't like the theory behind gun ownership. I agree that someone who breaks into my house loses all rights on whether he leaves with a few bullet holes in his spleen, and the slogan, "Guns don't kill people, people kill people" is something I can stand behind, even volunteering to wave the banner during a redneck rally. But, Rob has no experience with shooting a gun. Now that my cat's tail has narrowly missed amputation, I think this deserves a little reflection, which Rob tells me I can do while we are in the car on the way to buy the gun.

The gun shop is located in an upscale mall with shops for Armani, Tommy Hilfiger, and other high end lines. Who would think in the middle of Central America you could have access to such luxury? As we walk around looking for the gun shop, I notice that Rob clipped a can of mace, as one might clip a ballpoint pen, to the collar of his shirt. He thinks it makes him look scary, an observation reinforced by the expression on every salesperson's face as we enter their store.

"Will you please take that off? You look like a nut. Seriously, is that how you're going to walk into a gun store?" A minute passes before turning back around and catching Rob accidentally macing himself in the eye. He has now succeeded in looking like the scariest person in the mall.

"I've got to get to a bathroom; it's burning really bad," Rob says as the surrounding tissue of his eye begins to simmer. We find the food court and he disappears in the men's room for half an hour. I enjoy the alone time and eat a slice of pizza; not surprisingly, it tastes like a taco. He exits the bathroom, and his eye is puffier and redder than before. I suggest skipping the gun store, but Rob insists he's going to buy a firearm today.

The gun shop has numerous glass display cases with a large selection of hunting knives, nunchucks, and batons. Above the cases, a harpoon and AK-47 are mounted side-by-side on the wall. It's an admirable inventory, one that any manslaughter enthusiast would applaud. I'm looking at ten years to life for just walking into this store.

We walk up to the counter and see the salesman buzz something hidden beneath him; consequently, another man walks from the back and stands in the corner, watching us. The salesman requests our paperwork: a criminal report and a separate corporation for the gun. Everything you own in Costa Rica goes into a corporation for legal purposes I still don't quite understand. Even my cell phone is in a corporation. Since my husband has never operated a gun, he's prepared a list of absurd questions. I take a seat next to a rotating stand of Zippo lighters, knowing, from past experiences with Rob, this is going to be more entertaining than the Macy's Thanksgiving Day Parade.

"Will it shoot underwater?" Rob asks.

"Sir, why would you be underwater with your gun? I would suggest the harpoon," he says while pointing to it on the wall.

"What about fire? If I was in a burning building, and the gun caught fire, would it shoot?"

"I would suggest if you were in a burning building you find the nearest exit and get out immediately."

"Ah ha... so you're saying it will not shoot?"

"No, the gun will shoot under high temperatures. Of course, if the bullets catch fire, they will explode... hey... what's happening to your eye?"

Rob's eye starts to squirt like a malfunctioning sprinkler system. The man in the corner runs into the back room and leaves his buddy alone to deal with Rob. It occurs to me that I should always carry a video camera when taking my husband out in public.

We end up purchasing a Smith & Wesson, or Saturday Night Special, or something with an equally badass name. Rob also buys a quick loader just in case five bullets aren't enough to kill the grizzly-sized intruder we'll catch peeing in my basil planter. I guide Rob out of the store since he is now temporarily blind in one eye and has lost all depth perception. The door automatically locks as we leave, and I don't blame them one conjunctivitis bit.

The only thing worse than buying a gun with Rob is watching him search for the perfect hiding place. While he scouts for a spot, I go into the bedroom, only to come back and find Rob sitting in the fireplace, his legs poking straight out with his upper torso hidden in the chimney. He's decided that hiding the gun up there is the safest place. I think hiding Rob up there is the safest place.

"What are we going to do if you forget it's there and we start a fire?"

"That will never happen. I'll always remember to take the gun down before starting a fire. It's the best hiding place we have so far. Remember, I am doing all this because I want you to be safe."

What a sweet thing to say, and to show his main goal in life is keeping me safe, he surprises me a few days later by forgetting to take the gun down before starting a fire.

"This is so nice and cozy. Where did you put the gun?" I ask Rob a second before we both see the gun drop from the hiding place and into the middle of the flames.

It lands with the nozzle pointing straight at me.

I find myself frozen for an unconscionable amount of time, even though knowing by doing so, I face a highly unpleasant and messy outcome.

Rob pushes me aside and screams, "GET A COOKIE SHEET!"

I race to the kitchen to grab the metal tray and a wet towel.

"Oh God... oh God... it's gonna blow," I scream while quickly trying to recall what the salesman said. I can't remember if he told Rob it would shoot underwater, in a fire, or both.

"STAND BACK." Rob throws the wet towel on the fire and slides the pistol onto the cookie sheet. He runs into the kitchen, drops both into the sink, and turns on the cold water. He submerges the gun and watches as the rubber coating on the handle melts into a congealed, amoebic formation. A toxic mushroom cloud chases us out of the house and onto the back patio.

While the black smoke fills the kitchen, Rob turns to me and says, "Well, you don't see that every day."

You're right Rob... no... I can't say I do.

To prove the gun still works after it has cooled and dried, Rob walks past the beeping alarms, over the fallen banana tree, and down to the river. He blasts three bullets into the ground, subsequently blasting three holes in our water pipes. The gun functions. Our water pressure doesn't.

What have I learned about this debacle? Three things: a gun will shoot while on fire and after being submerged underwater; Rob's stupid questions at the store eventually did serve a purpose, and gun practice is best done two hundred feet away from any utility lines.

Thankfully, he didn't buy the harpoon.

Residency, Jehovah Neighbor, & Italian Parts

I don't quite understand how electricity works, but I am guilty of taking it for granted. Small offenses like leaving the television on after walking out of a room or staring repeatedly in my refrigerator for something to eat were never a problem in the States. Outlets were always grounded, and my little electrical world was abundantly filled with lots of reliable overhead lighting and iced cold Dr. Pepper. I remember those fond days with the tenderness one might have of their first summer romance.

It is unclear who wired this house, but surely it could not have been a licensed electrician. He must have called in sick, so the builder used the landscaper to finish the job. There are absolutely no grounded outlets, not one. This morning, I foolishly wanted to make toast during a storm; a surge came through, zapping the appliance and launching my flaming bread two feet in the air. It was an incredible production only outdone by the incendiary crumbs dissipating across the floor and burning my socks. There is no better way to watch your toaster bite the dust and ignite your feet simultaneously.

Another thing that you don't usually see in the States is here, people steal electricity. They jimmy-rig cables and create a connection from the high voltage lines to a pole on the top of their house. When I first witnessed a guy doing this, I wanted to applaud the man, give him a well-deserved standing ovation after tossing him a bouquet of carnations. He's the guy you can rely on when you need a job done. What's a few zillion volts to your head when your fiancée wants to watch the *Real Housewives of San Jose*? Bravo, Sir... bravo.

It's strange to live in a place where you can't even count on the utilities, but on the flip side, it does keep you focused on the more important things. I don't have time to scrutinize every wrinkle on my face when I need to figure out why we haven't had water for eight hours. In fact, periodically shutting off the water or giving a well-deserved electrical surge to the American public would definitely keep them off their anxiety medication. Who cares if your mother-in-law is coming to stay for a week if you are busy extinguishing a fiery crock-pot? It's just a matter of priorities.

It also explains why people are so nice here. They don't sweat the small stuff, and they focus on the present moment instead of obsessing over the past or future. Valuing what is mundane in your life, not just the spectacular, might be the long sought key to happiness. Something as simple as turning on your faucet and seeing clean water should make you ecstatic each and every day. This is another lesson I've learned since moving here. It took an exploding toaster and first degree burns to convince me.

Happiness and a carefree attitude do not come naturally to some people, including me. Nevertheless, I have found that small moments of appreciation every day have helped me morph into a friendlier and kinder person. I'm not looking outward as much as I'm just being grateful for the things in life that I ordinarily would have overlooked. When I plug in my coffee maker and it doesn't catch on fire, I am generally in a better mood. It's still unclear why it took such a drastic move to a foreign country to turn me back into someone you might actually enjoy sitting with and having a cup of coffee. Not once since moving here have I wanted to punch Rachael Ray in the face, or anyone else for that matter, not even Dolores. Something is changing in me, and it's solely because of this little piece of paradise in the middle of Central America. I am convinced that this slower rhythm the Ticos are accustomed to will not only help me live longer, but has changed how I view the smallest things around me. Applying for permanent residency seems like the next logical step in becoming part of the community and making my stay here official.

I will have to rely on this new improved attitude since historically this process would even test the patience of the Dalai Lama. Rob found an attorney, Senor Guarvez, who will help us with residency for four hundred dollars apiece. Considering the amount of work involved, this seems like a good price. Not many attorneys will do these assignments since the immigration office is notorious for losing your files. You then have to start the whole process over again. Getting residency sounds like as much fun as buying a car in Costa Rica.

On the flip side of this arduous process, I do like Guarvez. He is soft spoken and raised on the Caribbean side of Costa Rica. He enjoys telling us stories about how boring it was growing up swimming, snorkeling, and savoring lazy picnics on the beach. It seems like a great life, but he has wanderlust for one day living in New York City. This, of course, makes Rob cringe. The choice between snorkeling in the Caribbean or knocking rats out of your garbage cans is not a hard one to make. I suppose it is all a matter of perception: Guarvez wants to be in the middle of the hustle and bustle, while Rob desperately fought to get out.

Guarvez gives us the list of the paperwork we need to file for residency, and from what I can see, this is going to be an ambitious project. We have to prove, in multiple ways, who we are. Papers need to be authorized, then notarized at the Secretary of State, and then again stamped at the Costa Rica Embassy in Washington DC. I gather this will not go smoothly since the last time I went to renew my driver's license in New Jersey they told me I didn't exist. This resulted in me spending three months proving that I did. Even airlines frequently take me out of their lines for questioning. One time at Zurich Airport, I was removed out of a security checkpoint and brought to a private room by a six foot Swiss woman. Panic raced through my body when I realized I was being questioned for transporting narcotics, a fearful situation that invites the bladder to handsomely empty and thoroughly wet oneself. It appears proving who I am, and that I am not an incontinent drug mule, is a full time job.

But, without residency, we have to leave the country every ninety days for seventy-two hours. Our visa expires soon, so we must plan a trip to fulfill our legal requirements to stay here. Many gringos drive south to Panama or north to Nicaragua, all depending on how adventurous they are. It's approximately an eight-hour car ride to Panama, so we choose to drive there first. Nicaragua will have to wait. I hope that I can figure out how to unlock the car radio, or I will be stuck listening to Rob sing the entire Beastie Boys catalogue, and believe me, it is impressively lengthy.

Guarvez calls and explains we need to meet him in town tomorrow to go to the San Jose Police Station for fingerprinting. We don't know any Spanish, so he will come to help translate. As I put the phone back down on the receiver, I look out the window and see a family moving into Jim the Jehovah's Witness' house. Jim told us he was planning to rent the house to a nice religious family from Minnesota. I didn't know if this was true since Jim frequently tells lots of conflicting stories, most concerning what he does for a living. So far, his stories include working as a city construction worker, a big shot tech guy at a big shot computer company, and the vaguest profession of all, an importer/exporter. I don't mind listening since he serves me coffee and Oreos while pontificating on his extraordinary accomplishments. I can listen to just about anything if you're serving me cookies.

"Hey Rob... someone is moving in next door."

"Don't go over there," he comments as I am already walking out the door with Clementine.

Rob thinks I am just being nosey, but my dog needs her walk. What's the crime in finding out who our new neighbors are? It's not like I am going to peek in their windows, an activity I reserve for when I am absolutely certain no one is home.

If there was a call from Central Casting looking for a family to replicate a Norman Rockwell painting, this one would get the part. There are two girls chasing butterflies and three boys throwing a baseball around. All the children are neatly dressed: the boys in Dockers, and the girls in pretty blue dresses. This juxtaposes harshly against my sweatpants and ripped T-shirt, a disheveled appearance that conveys more of a predator vibe than a friendly neighbor. I turn to walk away, but the parents come outside to introduce themselves.

Julie and Mark are by far the friendliest couple I have ever met, probably because they are from Minnesota. Think about it. How many people from Minnesota have you gotten into an altercation with in your life? That's right... none. Even their odd sing-songy Scandinavian accent is as cute as can be. They explain how they want their children to experience living in another country so they decided to relocate for a few years.

"Wow, it's going to be real adventure for your family," I say.

"Ya," Mark says.

"You betcha," Julie adds.

Listening to them makes my New Jersey accent sound like I'm in the waste management business.

I have to hand it to them. Moving to a foreign country is one thing, but moving with your entire family takes a lot of guts. Julie is going to continue to work as an accountant so long as she has a high-speed Internet connection, something Jim said was not a problem. I didn't give her the news yet that you can't count on Jim to tell you anything truthful. Even after fighting to get a high-speed connection, it frequently goes off throughout the day and sometimes doesn't work at all. The power situation also complicates the issue. I'd rather not assault her with the quirks of living here just yet since she will find all this out soon enough.

"What's with the padlock on the gate?" she asks. "Jim told us it would be fixed."

I consider whether I should fill her in on the "next Friday" excuses. The newest one includes Carlos telling me he is waiting for an electronic chip from Italy. Well, of course. How silly of me to ask. Waiting for a part from Italy makes perfect sense. Those crafty Italians are famous for not only cannoli and aqueducts, but also for innovations in hydraulic gate technology. I wanted to ask Carlos why he didn't just go to the store in town and buy a new electronic chip, but I feared it would embarrass him by exposing the little white lies he graciously entertains me with week after week. Before I can tell any of this to Julie, I see five dogs walk up the road. Dolores is not far behind.

"You're never going to believe what happened to me," she spouts while heading toward us. "I was walking in the other development, and the people kept telling me to keep out. I told them to shove it, so the next day a woman came, threw a glass of wine at me, and then punched me in the face." She reaches up to touch a small red mark on her cheek. "And then I got robbed! They took my walking stick and threw it in the forest. I'm going back to find it. I don't give a damn if they try to stop me."

If there were a contest, one that rewards a person for being the most bizarre, Dolores would consistently take first place. Her shelves would be gloriously lined with ribbons and her curio cabinets full of trophies. The other contestants would drop out unceremoniously once they realized they were competing against such a professional.

"Do you think that's a good idea?" I ask. "If she hit you, and then threw your walking stick, why would you go back there unless your strategy is to stop the punches with your face again?"

Dolores pauses, looks up in the air (something she is prone to do when I say anything with a lick of sense), and then skirts the question

127

by asking if Rob is home. She walks away without waiting for an answer.

"Who's that?" Julie asks.

I give her the short version of my weird dealings with Dolores, fearing Julie will question my lack of judgment for befriending her.

We watch Dolores walk up the hill and ambush Rob while he is working in his greenhouse. He's going to have to deal with her on his own. We have both adopted a "save yourself" survival strategy one might use when confronted by a herd of stampeding elephants. Everyone is on their own when it comes to Dolores.

I can see Julie and her family have a lot of unpacking to do, so I politely excuse myself and walk down the mountain. With Dolores talking to Rob, there is no reason to rush back to the house. After a long hike, I return to see Rob in his rocking chair staring out at the flowerbeds. It's common for someone to lapse into a catatonic state after an hour of listening to Dolores and watching her pee in the bushes.

"The new neighbors are from Minnesota. Isn't that nice? They seem really sweet, and I wasn't being nosey at all."

"Wasn't the movie *Fargo* filmed in Minnesota? That was about a bunch of murderers."

"Impossible, they can't be murderers. They were wearing Dockers. Psychopaths don't wear pleated, khaki pants."

However, I pause and consider the chances that my nicely dressed Jehovah's Witness neighbors are some kind of renegade criminals. You never know; it seems that everyone here has a story to tell, and maybe my nice Norman Rockwell family are really fugitives from the law. Maybe I'm getting too laid back and losing my pessimistic edge. Now that I think of it, their accent does sound a little suspicious.

You betcha it does.

Fingerprinting, Mean People,
& Rob's New Girlfriend

It is a fascinating sociological experiment watching how I relate to people compared to Rob. For one, he has absolutely no fear talking with people who don't understand him. Rob will play a prolonged game of charades until the person can figure out what he wants. His Brooklyn accent doesn't help with the translation, an accent that has become increasingly thicker since he quit work.

My favorite is at Burger King when he tells the cashier he wants the food to go. He pretends to wrap and then throw a present over his shoulder. It is advantageous that Costa Ricans are much more laid back than people in the States. Sometimes, the people standing in line participate like they are at a performance of *Tony n' Tina's Wedding*. They play along and yell out suggestions on what Rob is trying to communicate. It always ends with the group laughing at us or along with us, I can never tell which. Either way, Rob always gets what he needs. Unfortunately, I don't have his ability to go with the flow. I am more like a large piece of ice lodged in the middle of a river. I eventually melt and flood the whole damn town.

When I attempt to shop or pay bills in Costa Rica, the only thing I am successful at is inconveniencing the people around me. I have unnerved people who work at Motor Vehicles, and the phone and electric companies. Bank tellers are my favorite. I freeze when they ask me questions, remaining in a cryogenic state for at least two minutes before answering back. One time, the teller told me to have a wonderful day. I returned her comment by panicking and running away. I make friends wherever I go.

Maybe I feel this way because physically I don't blend in here. My lighter skin and blue eyes immediately give away that I am a foreigner. Rob tans easily and looks and acts like he could belong anywhere in the world: on the side of the road in Mexico eating a tamale, drinking an espresso while watching the World Cup in Italy, or on a pilgrimage to Mecca (by his seventh walk counterclockwise around the Ka'bah, someone would have already invited him over to their house for the traditional head shaving). On the other hand, I always have an expression on my face like I walked out the wrong door at Madison Square Garden. This quizzical look apparently translates into someone who will most likely monopolize an abundance of your time, and I won't even do it in your native language.

Today, we are going with our lawyer to get fingerprinted at the police station in San Jose. This feels like we are putting the cart before the horse, or more accurately for Costa Rica, the oxcart before the ox. We just started the process, so I don't understand why they need our fingerprints. However, the lawyer tells my husband we need to get this done before our appointment at immigration. That's another thing. There is an underlining *machismo* thing going on here. When the lawyer calls, or our land surveyor, or anyone who has something that requires a conversation of more than two syllable words, they only want to talk with Rob. This is ironic because Rob works diligently in avoiding polysyllabic conversations. This diligence even surpasses his refusal to wear pants during the day. So, how do I feel about the obvious sexism I encounter with these men? I really don't care. I took on so many things while we ran our businesses, I can let him handle some responsibility for a while. Rob handling it in his underwear is of no great sacrifice to me.

We are driving out of the development to meet with our attorney when we run into Carlos. "*Pura Vida*," he yells over his weed whacker. He takes off his beehive headgear and walks over to our car. I tell him we are driving to the police station in San Jose and will be back later in the day.

"*No... no bien*," Carlos says, shaking his head like a disapproving father. He reaches into his pocket and draws his finger out like a gun. "Bang bang," he shouts.

"Holy crap...what the hell does that mean?" I say to Rob.

Carlos then reaches into his back pocket and takes out his wallet. We watch as he goes into an entertaining production of cops and robbers, one man holding a gun while sticking up the other poor schmuck. I think we are the other poor schmuck. Carlos returns his wallet to his back pocket, says some more things in Spanish, and walks away.

"Wow, I guess he is warning us to be careful, but why the theatrics when we are going to the *police station*? Is that really necessary?"

Rob doesn't answer my question, instead clipping a can of pepper spray to his shirt.

The police station is in the middle of San Jose, a city where the streets have no names. The blocks are positioned in no coherent order. Some wind around into one-ways, then wind back into dead ends. It is impossible for me to keep track or to remember how to get back here if the need arises. The attorney points to a huge building and tells us to park across the street.

We walk to the police station entrance, where an armed officer is standing. He checks our bags, scans us with a metal detector, and radios other officers when he sees Rob's pepper spray. Before Rob gets thrown in the slammer (not a good place for a man who doesn't like to wear pants), the attorney does some fast talking. The officer smiles, takes the can, and gives Rob a numbered tag identical to what you would get from an attendant in a coatroom. It's nice to know you can check your pepper spray at the door.

I am shocked at all the police at the station, mainly because I rarely see any police. Evidently, they are all here. This must be the most secure place in Costa Rica. My attorney takes us to a walk-up window, and an officer hands us a small form to complete. He then points for us to sit outside. There are chairs lined up against the building, really crappy ones that you would see in a really crappy waiting room. It appears the same medical exam office decorator was called in for this project, as well. The chairs are grubby, so I choose to sit atop a three foot high brick wall. I let my legs dangle while my attorney fills out the paper. I watch as the officer directs more people to sit in the plastic chairs; the sun is beaming directly on them. They move, but the officer yells out for them to sit back down. The men and women hold up files in front of their faces to block the sun. I don't even glance at the officer in case he is going to reprimand me, too.

Ten minutes later, the officer calls out our names, and we walk inside the building. I look back, and the man tells our lawyer he can't come in with us. This unnerves me because a police station is not the place where you want things that you say misinterpreted. The officer sees my distress and points for me to keep walking. I let Rob take the lead and look back at my attorney as if it is the last time I will ever see him, or my freedom, again.

The room is filled with computer stations and individual chairs to the left side of each desk. There are about ten desks in all. I look around, and the place resembles an elementary class—that's if your schoolroom just went through a hurricane, followed by an earthquake, and ended in a high profile hostage shootout. Discolored plaster hides the cracks and holes in the wall. The linoleum tiles are either broken or missing all together. On the back wall is shelving filled with dozens of three ring binders. I notice one of the binders shows more wear and tear than the rest. The label reads "sexual offenders", and like a popular library book, the corners are folded over and heavily leafed through. To think: I put People magazines in my office for my patients to browse through.

We are directed to sit on a wooden bench against the wall. With each person called, Rob and I slide down the bench, until I am the next one up. A woman gets up from behind a desk and walks over to me. She is in her late forties, wearing a purple shirt, purple pants, and five-inch purple stilettos. I know that if this woman woke up this morning and knowingly dressed herself like this, I don't stand a chance. She points to me and asks if I speak Spanish. I tell her only a little, causing her to erupt into a raging fit. Her face turns a shade that matches the color of her shirt, and she walks out into the hall to holler some more.

Another heavyset woman of similar age walks over to Rob. She smiles wide, takes him by the elbow, and they walk away arm in arm. He tells her he only speaks a little Spanish, and unlike the doll face that is helping me, she tells him not to worry; she will take good care of him. He sits down at her workstation, and the first thing she does is lean in and ask what color his eyes are. Are you kidding me? She then asks if he is married. Rob glances back at me and gives a thumbs up. He quickly turns around once he sees the Flying Purple People Eater plop back down in front of me. He too is frightened of her.

I give her the paper the attorney had already filled out for me. She tosses it aside and starts entering information on her computer. She asks how much I weigh. I quickly try to convert to the metric system and tell her I weigh thirty-five kilograms, which I later realize is seventy-eight pounds. She stares at me, looks me up and down, and enters it into her computer. She then asks how tall I am. Behind her is a wall with measurements scribbled onto it, similar to something you would see in a family's kitchen with children's heights recorded year after year. I suspect this must be the right place to measure myself, so I jump up and stand next to it like a dummy. I see that the measurements start at one centimeter, and unless the criminals here are a bunch of Smurfs, I can't fathom why the chart starts so low. I continue leaning against the wall until she signals me to come back. She records my height as 177 centimeters, which would make me a lovely five foot eight, eight inches taller than I actually am. So at this height and seventy-eight pounds, I am quite the stunner.

Back to "Days of Our Lives" at the other desk, Rob's lady is giggling at everything he says. Once she hears he is a chiropractor, she offers to trade him Spanish lessons for a shoulder massage, *wink...wink*. I am surprised she hasn't poured him a glass of wine and pulled out a Barry White CD.

Purple Lady is now talking really slowly to me. She is exaggerating her lips, and I am waiting for her to grab my hands like Helen Keller and put them against her mouth. She keeps asking me *color... color?* while moving her lips really slowly. I get it... color, but color of what? What the hell does she want? Thinking she is asking about my eyes, I take my glasses off, lean in close, and scramble my eyes around wildly. She quickly jumps back. She now thinks I am crazy and orders for someone to come over. While I'm still flailing my eyeballs around in my head, a man asks me in English what color my house is. I regain my focus and tell the man my house is yellow, which it is not, more like a charming Burnt Sienna, but how can I possibly explain that? She never did get around to asking me the color of my eyes. I am sure the thirty seconds of me gawking at her like the Unabomber gave her plenty of time to figure it out.

While all this happens, surprisingly, I don't get too frazzled. I just know it is not going my way, and Purple Lady is going to make it as hard for me as she can. As my friend Scott would say, my ass is in the wind. Wisely, I sit back and get my tail end handed to me because if the tables were turned, on a bad day, I might have equally had a similar attitude. I don't blame her one bit for her temperament. I want to reach over, put my arms around her violet shoulders, and tell her, "Really, Lady, it's not you, it's me. I get it that you have a two-hour siesta coming up and those five-inch purple stilettos are definitely made for walking, so holler all you want. Scream and shout. I will still be here, but let's make one thing clear. Although I am new to your country and have not yet mastered your language, I would never be caught dead in that outfit. An entire purple outfit has never worked on anyone except Grimace, so let's bang the rest of this out without any more tantrums." I want to say all that, but I don't know how, and anyway I'm too distracted watching another woman caress my husband's forearm.

After an hour of entering my personal information into the Costa Rican data bank, she tells me to split, and I am more than happy to oblige. She points to a female officer, and I go and get fingerprinted. Before I leave, I glance back at Rob. I think his lady just invited him over for Christmas.

The officer who is taking my fingerprints is on her cell phone with her boyfriend. Thankfully, her boyfriend is not breaking up with her, so she barely looks at me and doesn't give me any attitude. She takes a roller, covers it in a pad of ink, and then rolls it over a piece of metal. While talking on the phone, she grabs my hands and pushes them down on the piece of metal, blackening all my fingers. She also goes the extra mile and does my palms, too. Next, she pushes my fingers onto a piece of beige cardboard and tosses it into a disheveled pile. She hands me back one small piece of paper with my thumbprint on it. I walk outside, wash my hands at a communal sink, and head toward my attorney.

Rob struts out fifteen minutes later.

"Not so bad," he says. "That was the easiest thing I've done so far in Costa Rica."

We walk back to the officer at the gate, and Rob gives him the number for his pepper spray. The officer cleverly hands it over to him in this weird way: he reaches around his back and secretly palms it over to Rob.

"I've lived long enough in New York to know that was a real fishy way he just passed this to me," Rob comments. "That guy has definitely done some questionable stuff."

The officer gives us a farewell smile and lifts the gate for us to leave.

On the ride back, the car in front of us puts on its brakes.

"Is that a toilet in the road?" Rob asks.

We drive a little farther and see that a Porta-Potty fell off a truck, hit the hood of a car, and splattered all over a motorcyclist. So in the end, compared to that guy, I guess my day at the precinct wasn't so bad.

It's good to know that I've officially started my residency process, and I am in the system. I hope that I won't have to go through the fingerprinting process again. I do have a good cover if I ever commit a crime here: they will be looking for my alter ego, the five foot eight, seventy-eight pound version of me. Rob will never have to worry about getting arrested; in fact, I bet his new girlfriend never even put his information in the computer. It's only a matter of time before she arrives on our doorstep... you know, to teach him Spanish... *wink, wink.*

Dolores' Graveyard

Recovering from driving into San Jose always takes a couple of days. It feels good we started the beginning stages of our residency process, but fear it's just the beginning to a long and difficult process. Many gringos in Costa Rica don't ever bother to do it and just leave the country every ninety days. I want to be here legally and can't imagine doing that for the next ten years. I'm all up for an adventure, but the thought of driving all over Central America just to get our visa renewed is too much stress for me.

I'm about to look over the many forms my attorney gave me when I am interrupted by a phone call from Dolores. She is crying that a car fatally hit one of her dogs. The bad news doesn't surprise me. For someone who loves and rescues dogs, Dolores is pretty careless. She doesn't use a leash, lead, or even confine her dogs to her yard. They run freely in the road, so this was bound to happen. In between the sobbing, she asks if Rob will help bury the dog. I turn to ask him, and as always, he agrees. Rob's heart is as big as the ocean is deep. Even though he almost broke his leg saving her bird, he knows a sixty-year-old lady should not be digging a six foot hole in sweltering heat. He has one stipulation: he does not want to see the dog. He just wants to do all the digging and get the hell out of there. She agrees, and I tell her we will be there after we get back from doing a few errands.

I knock on Dolores' door and hear hollering from the other side.

"You don't knock in Costa Rica; you say, *'Con permiso'.*"

I yell out, *"Con permiso."*

She still doesn't open the door.

This is profoundly annoying because Dolores doesn't repeat this when she comes uninvited to my home. In fact, she doesn't even knock on my door. Every morning Dolores marches to my house and stares directly in my living room window while I watch *Everybody Loves Raymond* in my pajamas. I am sure her five dogs would stare, too, if they weren't already busy whizzing all over my yoga mat and the clean laundry hanging on my clothesline.

"Just open the damn door, Dolores," I bark back.

She opens it and questions why it took us so long.

I ask if I can keep my ice cream sandwiches I just bought at the store in her freezer while Rob digs the hole.

She hems and haws, saying there isn't enough room. I show her how small they are, and she finally concedes. I open her freezer, move over a Ziploc plastic bag, and place my ice cream underneath it.

We walk outside to her backyard where there are little stone markers dotted throughout the lawn. We carefully step over graves while Dolores yells.

"Don't dig there; that's where I buried Bingo. Don't step here, oh, poor little Snowball, and dear Squeaky is next to her."

Apparently, all of God's creations, every one that marched off Noah's Ark, are buried behind Dolores' house. Rob cross-examines her, wants to make sure when he starts to dig he does not find one of her pets. While she is deciding, I leave her with my grave-digging husband and walk back to the house.

After I take a seat on her sofa, she comes back inside and offers me a cup of coffee. She sits down and discloses in a whispered voice, a tone that would suggest we are being wiretapped, that she can't find her calculator.

"It's been missing since the Indian spirits stole it."

I lightly cover my mouth (just in case these eavesdroppers have sophisticated lip reading technology... and because I'm feeling like Agent 99) and ask her how she can be so certain Indian spirits snuck into her house on a Saturday afternoon. Maybe they yelled *con permiso* first, and she wasn't home.

"I know they took it because they stole the second one I had in the drawer two days ago."

For one nanosecond, my mind thinks *Hey, she makes perfect sense* before I rush back into consciousness and realize if I spend any more time with her my head might explode.

Despite my objections, Dolores tells a story of how her house is built over an Indian burial ground.

I question why the spirits want calculators, because from my previous knowledge about Indians, I am certain they are not busy doing quarterly tax reports. I am all but positive they wouldn't pull out a Texas Instruments calculator to rectify a situation. What I don't mention, and what you have already been thinking, is she is repeating the storyline from the movie *Poltergeist*.

She explains this is irrefutable proof she has bad luck. The pissed off Indian spirits seek revenge by making it impossible for her to add and multiply correctly.

I consider that if the bad luck only resulted in stolen calculators, it's not so crummy. I would gladly offer my calculators and would even throw in my iPod if it would keep them from haunting me.

She doesn't have a chance to answer. We hear Rob shouting, "Dolorrreeeessss".

We run out and see Rob standing over the grave.

"I thought you told me nothing was buried here." Through gritted teeth, Rob takes the shovel and lifts up a small white garbage bag with something rotting inside.

"Maybe it's the missing calculators?" I chime in.

They both ignore me.

"You forgot you buried something here," Rob grunts.

Dolores looks up to the sky for answers.

"No," she replies. "Someone must have slipped into my backyard and buried it. Just put it on the grass over here."

Rob tosses the bag to the side and digs farther. The deeper he goes, the more his face turns red.

I consider it is possible Rob might have a heart attack from all this exertion. Ironically, he would fall over dead in the grave he just dug; subsequently sharing a headstone with a dog named Snickerdoodles. Since I don't want to see Dolores every time I visit my husband's grave, I run to get a glass of cold water and pour it over the back of his neck.

Finally, it's time to lay the dog in her final resting place. Dolores returns with a pair of hedge clippers along with the animal wrapped in a sheet. "I want you to cut off her tail before you bury her."

"Huh... what?" Rob says. He continues in a consoling voice, "Why would you want to do that... are you sure... let's think about this. What are you going to do with it... use it as a key chain?"

Initially, I think that's perfectly reasonable. As a kid, I received a rabbit foot key chain in my goody bag at Tilly Goldstein's sixth birthday party. I loved the soft fur and used to pet it throughout the school day, keeping it in the front pocket of my dungarees for easy access. It was only a couple years later I realized I was petting a petrified amputated appendage. In a Greenpeace display of activism, I threw the rabbit's foot in the cafeteria garbage can and gave a lengthy but heartfelt denunciation on animal cruelty to a table of horrified second graders.

I repeat this story to Dolores as she sharpens the hedge clipper blades.

She briefly pauses when I also remind her she does not want to anger the calculator-stealing gods any further. This last detail appears to convince her, and she agrees to let Rob bury the dog with her tail.

Rob takes the dog and places her into the grave.

Dolores recites a lengthy eulogy. When she finishes, Rob picks up the white plastic bag with the mystery animal inside and puts it into the hole.

She screams and wants him to dig another grave for the other animal. Without acknowledging anything she just said, Rob tosses more dirt on top of both animals and fills the hole.

Back in her kitchen, I open the freezer to get my ice cream. The plastic Ziploc bag slides out of the freezer, and I catch it mid-air before it hits the floor. In my hand is a frozen wild bird. Once a beautiful blue and green Mot Mot, it visited Dolores every morning until she found it dead on her porch. She then stuck it in her freezer; that was two years ago. We have had at least half a dozen blackouts since then, so I can only imagine how many times this bird has been thawed out then frozen again during the past two years. I also consider the safety of my ice cream sandwiches that have been sitting underneath it. Instead of asking what the rest of the plastic bags in her freezer contain, we figure there would be plenty more holes to dig, so we decide to keep the conversation short and head on home.

I'm not sure what the strangest part of the story is: the pet cemetery, Indian poltergeists, or the frozen bird. Or, maybe it's that my husband ate all the ice cream sandwiches that night while watching The History Channel. There is no way around dealing with Dolores. No matter what I do, she will be a part of my life here. I hope the Indian spirits will give her back her calculators and she finds some peace.

I didn't bother telling Dolores there is a calculator application on her computer. It's only a matter of time before the Indian spirits figure that out and it disappears as well.

Part III

Drowning Seems To Be The Hardest Part

It's time to drive to Panama and renew our ninety day visa. I have a lot of anxiety about this trip since it will be my first drive across a border into a foreign country. My family drove across the border into Canada when I was a kid, but that was about as exciting as a game of Mad Libs, and can you really consider Canada a perilous border? It's more like a distant cousin you think about occasionally but rarely make the effort to visit.

We just learned we need special paperwork from the National Registry in San Jose that will allow us to drive our car out of the country. It's irritating to know that I moved to a country that requires grown-ups to get something equivalent to a hall pass. If you don't have the proper documentation, the officials at the border will not let you take your car across and possibly have the authority to send you to your room without dinner.

Not surprisingly, we get lost while trying to find the government building. We eventually find it tucked inside a shopping mall next to a chandelier store. I've been diligent in studying Spanish and show off my ability of combining both a noun and verb in one sentence. Even though I have the grammatical skills of a two year old, my effort is reciprocated with smiles mainly because I appear a little mentally deficient (a condition supported by the fact that my glasses recently cracked at the bridge of my nose and are stuck together with electrical tape). This sexy look actually causes people to spend more time helping me.

I explain my situation to the clerk. She hands me eight stamps and tells me to use a wet sponge on the table in the corner to affix them to the paper. She waves her finger in the air in an attempt to show me that I should not place my tongue on the stamp to wet it. Got it; I've seen what happened when George Costanza ordered the cheap wedding invitations.

People stand around the table and slosh their stamps on the communal Staphylococcus sponge before sticking them to their forms. The sponge overly saturates my stamps and drenches my paper with dirty water. The clerk instructs me to stand in one of the many lines with my soggy paper until someone is ready to help me. It's easy to look dim witted when these are my marching orders.

It's my turn so I walk up to the window and hand the woman my car registration and newly stamped form. She takes my paperwork, grabs a big wooden handle, and stamps it into an ink blotter. She spends the next two minutes covering my paperwork with thirty official looking blue circles. She stamps like she has a grudge, like her boyfriend just told her he wants to take a break conveniently before his vacation to Cancun. She finally hands them back to us underlining the paragraph that allows us to take our car out of the country within the next thirty days. This important accomplishment feels largely uneventful. I walk back to the car, stick the papers in the glove compartment, and hope it was everything we need for our trip.

It's nerve racking to know most gringos won't drive their car across the border. They find a place to park (which is usually someone's front yard), walk across, and take a bus to their destination.

I would rather go through the headache and get the proper paperwork than risk my car stolen at the border.

"Doesn't this make you a little stressed?" I ask Rob.

"Not at all. Seriously, how hard can it be to drive to Panama? People do it every day so don't assume it's going to be difficult." Sometimes my husband's "can do" attitude can seriously get on my nerves. He's one of those perpetually upbeat people. Frankly, the type of person you would eat first while stranded in the Andes after a plane crash.

Instead of taking the Pan American Highway straight into Panama, Rob wants to travel across to the Caribbean first, spend a few days at the beach, then cross over the lesser used Panama border in a town named Sixaola. I'd rather take the Pan American highway but Rob insists that we should go to the Caribbean, do some snorkeling, and relax on the beach before heading into Panama. From there we can then travel to Bocas del Toro, a small group of islands in Panama with incredible marine life and mangroves. The only problem is I can't find much information about this border and am unsure if it is safe to cross there. However, it is hard to argue with Rob's idea to drive to the Caribbean. Who drives to the Caribbean? Just being able to say it makes me giddy. I abandon my plan, adopt a little of my husband's optimistic attitude, and decide to head off to the beach.

One highway takes us to the eastern coast but first we get lost driving through San Jose searching for it. We drive for about an hour, winding our way around the streets before finding the entrance to Highway 32. After twenty minutes, we find ourselves passing through a seriously dense national park called Braulio Carrillo. According to my guidebook, the rainforest is one hundred and eighteen thousand acres and is home to over six thousand species of plants and animals. It is eighty-five percent primary rainforest receiving one hundred seventy-five inches of rain per year. We just left the civilized world and entered the land of the lost.

The recklessly carved road in the mountainside has a bad reputation of being treacherous during the rainy season. It isn't uncommon for the road to close due to mudslides or large boulders crashing onto the road. I look up as we drive and see rocks precariously hanging onto the ridge. It looks like they are ready to tumble at any moment. Without missing a beat, I nag Rob by telling him we should have taken the Pan American highway.

Although it is a dangerous road, the park itself is a marvel. It's almost a vulgarity to know this roadway destroyed part of it. It is rare to see this amount of untouched forest. This place is a must for bird lovers; home to funny named ones like bare-neck umbrella birds, flame-throated warblers, and long-tail silky flycatchers. There have been sightings of jaguars, ocelots, white-faced capuchin monkeys, and tapirs. Overall, you definitely want to see this park when visiting Costa Rica, especially if you are in the business of giving birds silly sounding names.

Luckily, it is a dry day and the winding road takes us along the ridge of the mountain. I look over the side and notice if we drove off, most likely no one would ever find us. Our car would crash and be simultaneously swallowed by impenetrable vegetation, our injured bodies pecked to death by a hungry silky flycatcher. I consider finding a safe overlook to take a picture but before I do I grab my trusted Frommer's guide to read their section on this park:

"Be careful here. Make sure you park your car in and base your explorations from the park's main entrance, not just anywhere along the highway. There have been several robberies and attacks against visitors reported at trails leading into the park from the highway. This park also seems to have the highest incidence of lost hikers."

Lost hikers and armed robberies—a legendary combination. "Do you want to stop?" I ask Rob.

"Are you nuts? No way. Look around, the forest is so dense we're shit out of luck if we get lost." The park is very close to San Jose, which would explain how easy it is to commit a crime here. However, to put it in perspective, every park has some element of crime. Even in New York City's Central Park, unfortunate things happen to people who decide to take a jog through lesser-populated areas. Nevertheless, this park is not the rainforest, and the rainforest always gives you the eerie feeling you can disappear under the deep overgrowth never to be seen or heard from again. At the very least, someone holding a Vente Caramel Latte will eventually stumble across your decomposing body in Central Park. It's questionable whether that will happen here.

After four hours, we reach the Caribbean port of Limon and turn right to continue south down the coastal highway. The road gives a breezy view of the sea with the occasional Tico family picnicking on the sand. It's fantastic no one else is around. The last time I was at a New Jersey beach the corner of my towel touched the corner of my neighbor's towel. There wasn't even room to walk down to the ocean. The family I am watching today has an entire stretch of beach to themselves. I try to take a picture but Rob drives over a pothole causing the glove compartment to pop open. Out falls our Panama paperwork and a small piece of laminated plastic with a sequence of numbers. I punch the numbers into the car radio and out blasts Bob Marley through the speakers. This solves the annoying Scooby-Doo radio mystery and we celebrate by listening to relaxing sounds of reggae music over our stereo system.

Before we left, Rob made reservations in a small town called Punta Uva. The hotel on the beach, and more importantly, home of the best snorkeling in Costa Rica. His careful research discovered extensive coral formations only steps from the shoreline. Past volcanic activity produced a stretch of coral reef with deep twists and caverns. We quickly drop off our bags in our rooms and head off to the water with our snorkel gear.

With no one around, we snorkel in three feet of water and see an enormous variety of fish: tangs, angelfish, crabs, starfish, damsels, sergeant majors, and eels. Rob holds onto my elbow guiding me around as I float face down in the salty water. Thirty minutes later, I lift my head and notice we are very far away from the shore. It startles me and I instantly breathe in a mouthful of water. This is followed by a mouthful of panic as I quickly start to sink. Do you know how hard it is to sink in calm salty water when you already know how to swim? Really hard. You have to want to drown. Really put everything you got into it. I do not even take the snorkel out of my mouth. It is that bad.

Before the water covers my head for the last time, I yell for Rob to turn around. He sees me and instantly rips off his expensive new snorkel and mask, tossing it into the sea. He grabs me and tries to swim back to shore.

"Kick your legs," he screams. "For Christ's sake, you know how to swim, KICK YOUR LEGS." My mind switches from certain death to certain will to live. Suddenly, I get a surge of adrenaline. My limbs start to move and I swim as fast as I can to a piece of coral in a shallower spot in the water. I lean my knee onto it giving me a chance to take a few deep breaths with my head above the water.

"I found the hand of God," I cry (in my defense, I really thought I was going to die).

"Holy shit, what are you doing?" I hear Rob call from behind. Red water oozes to the surface while I try to stay on the rock. The coral slit my knee open and as blood surrounds me, quite instantly, a whole lot more fish do as well. "Keep going, don't stop. Get out of here." Rob again pushes me from behind. I never saw Rob scared of sharks but I have put us both in a very delicious position. We are now both marinating in a pool of blood. I finally make it back to the beach and collapse weeping on my towel. I bawl as Rob tends to my knee and tries to stop the bleeding. "What happened out there? You know how to swim."

"I panicked. Sorry about your mask and snorkel."

"I don't care about that. You really scared me to death." Rob wraps my knee and I can see his eyes water. This is the guy you should NOT eat first if stranded in the Andes Mountains. He would be the one who would save everybody after hiking a week in a blizzard to find help. In fact, someone should eat me first since I add nothing to an emergency except the impossible ability to sink in unsinkable salty water.

After my drowning disaster, Rob drives into town and buys a new snorkel set and a big blue flotation device that wraps around my entire body. This makes me float upright like a big blue buoy that, I have to admit, is quite enjoyable. As Rob swims looking for fish, I just float around like a Weeble Wobble exerting no energy at all. The only way it could get better is if I had a strawberry daiquiri in my hand. It appears drowning has introduced me to my new favorite activity.

The next two days we enjoy the beach and sunshine. I take Rob's advice and shed some of my anxiety. I decide that I need to stop anticipating the worst and welcome each new adventure without succumbing to my nerves. There is no reason to assume something bad will happen.

We pack up and drive a half hour to the border. The closer we get we can see what looks like a bridge that spans a busy river. A bridge that looks ten minutes away from collapsing.

Bridge Over Troubled Waters

This rickety connection between both countries used to be an old railroad bridge. It is too narrow to accommodate two-way traffic, so vehicles must take turns going over one at a time. The only thing preventing cars from crashing into the river below are planks of wood stretched out across the bridge, a design one would not expect to see at a border used by hundreds of tractor-trailers a day.

"That's it? How are we supposed to get across?" I watch as an eighteen-wheeler turns his high beams on and speeds across the bridge. Small planks of wood crack and splinter under its weight and pedestrians scatter to get out of the way.

"See, that guy wouldn't go over if it wasn't safe," Rob says with little confidence in his voice. However, even Mr. Optimism can't hide the fact that this bridge is ready to crumble any day now and it's our only way into Panama.

Several people approach us for translation services. For twenty dollars, they will get us to the front of the line and have our car papers stamped without any hassles. Rob picks a young guy named Javier who speaks relatively good English. He asks for copies of our registration but we realize we didn't make any. Rob goes off with Javier to a small bodega while I wait by the car.

The movie Midnight Express comes to mind when I look around at the dusty town. A film you rather not remember when traveling through a foreign country. This town looks like the perfect place one would tape several bricks of hashish across their chest and attempt to smuggle it across the border. I start to get nervous even though I have done nothing to get nervous about. It doesn't help that I just read about the prisons in Central America and concluded I don't want to spend any amount of time in one.

San Lucas Island was home to one of the most notorious and brutal prisons in Costa Rica. It was located off the shores of the Pacific coast and housed the worst criminals in the country, many of whom spent their years in solitary confinement. You can still see the graffiti on the walls of the cells often depicting their horrid conditions and desperation. It closed in 1991 and the government transformed it into a national park. I can't say it is as popular as Disney World but tourists come to walk the halls once used as torture tunnels. I can already hear little Alfonso now, "Este isn't Space Mountain—mi padres suck."

Rob and Javier walk back with the photocopies and we quickly get our passports and car papers stamped on the Costa Rican side. We climb back in the car and Javier tells us to turn the lights on. It's the universal sign for "Hey, it's my turn to cross this bridge so get the hell out of my way." I question him about the safety of the bridge but he tells me not to worry. The one-hundred year old bridge has not collapsed yet. Rob doesn't even look at me. Once again, I remind him we should have taken the Pan American Highway.

We drive up to the bridge but stop in front of a wooden board outstretched three feet above the road. This is the last checkpoint before leaving Costa Rica and the officials who are usually there to lift it are out to lunch (siestas are taken very seriously down here). I am willing to take matters into my own hands and lift it myself but I recall a prison scene from Midnight Express and wisely decide otherwise. Javier jumps out and finds a border patrol eating a sandwich. He hands the officer a couple bucks, the guy wipes a drop of mayonnaise off his face, and unenthusiastically lifts the board.

As we cross the bridge, we can hear the cracking of wood planks beneath our tires. Women carrying babies squeeze against the side to let us pass. Every time our wheel hits one of the metal rails in the middle of the bridge, it makes the tire ricochet back. I cover my face with my hands afraid we are going to crash into the water below. It is the longest I have ever held my breath, a physiological feat I need to repeat if I ever get caught drowning in the Caribbean again.

We make it to the other side where Javier tells us to hurry and roll up all our windows. A second later, anti-fungus banana insecticide sprays our car. I watch as the sudsy water washes our car and the many dirty barefoot backpackers walking past us. I have a tendency to romanticize the whole backpacker lifestyle. I always tell Rob how much fun it would be traveling with everything we need on our back. Before this trip, I rambled on and on about the thrill of backpacking across Central and South America. Rob takes this opportunity to point at the backpacker's dirty feet and lecture that I would *never* walk through an insecticide spray, I would *never* go days without showering, and just the idea of walking barefoot for ten minutes would have me flipping out. Plus, the backpack would be too heavy and *he* would end up carrying it. After the spray stops, I roll down my window and a barefoot backpacker walks past. The smell suspends itself in the air and hijacks my nasal passage. I thought the bridge was dangerous, but the smell of a backpacker who hasn't bathed in two weeks is lethal.

We are finally on the Panama side. We quickly pay a combined fee of ten dollars for our thirty-day visas and step to the next window to get our car papers stamped. This seems to be going surprisingly smoother than I expected. I am only one window away from getting out of this town and onward towards Bocas del Toro. My optimistic attitude deflates when the man behind the window yells at me and shakes my documents in the air. Javier just walked away and I can't understand what the man is screaming about. I tell him the official paperwork allows me to bring my car into the country. The guy points to the documents and tells me they are bad, very bad, like possibly the worst piece of shitty documentation that has ever passed his reputable desk. I once again point to my paper and show him the National Registry heading. I even point out my soggy stamps.

"Listen man, I got the stamps," I holler while pointing at the scribbly ink circles all over the page. He looks them over and shakes his head. I get increasingly agitated and yell, "STAMPS MAN, I GOT THE STAMPS." He does not wave me through. Instead, he swiftly tosses my passport and car papers over his shoulder. They land on an empty desk behind him and he demands I step aside for the next person.

I lose all peripheral vision and focus solely on my passport in the corner. But there is nothing I can do. I can't go anywhere without it and can't even drive our car back out of here. We are stuck at the Panama border with nothing to do but wait for a little mercy from the asshole behind the glass.

We wait. And wait. And wait. Javier says he doesn't understand the situation, but I do. I have some kind of evil curse attached to my passport. I get stopped everywhere we go, whether it be at an international airport or in a Central American border town.

After an hour, the man behind the glass reaches around and grabs my passport, stamps it, and returns my paperwork. The dust has mixed with my sweat and formed a crusty patina over my body. I resemble the backpackers walking past me. I am one of them now. I stink too.

We take off as quickly as possible just in case they decide to detain us any longer. Javier gives us a quick wave before walking back over the bridge to the Costa Rican side. I can pass through a place like this whereas Javier needs to stay.

I wonder how many times Javier does this a day. Watching him makes me reflect on my own life. It's all a matter of perspective but growing up in America is comparable to winning the lottery.

I feel lucky that I was born in the United States. You don't know how bad things are until you're stuck at a Central American border. And doesn't luck play the biggest role in where we end up in life? I'm still proud to be an American but now I acknowledge that I've been given opportunities few around the world get. All because my mother gave birth on American soil.

I watch Javier in the rear-view mirror. He once again approaches people like me looking to cross safely to the other side.

I'm glad I made it.

Nadine the Incompetent Explorer

There is no local ferry that can take our car from the mainland to the Bocas del Toro islands. Therefore, we have to park it at the local fire station where Rob turns on all three kill-switches, secures two Clubs to the steering wheel, and removes a plug to the battery. I fear whoever tries to steal our car will get so frustrated they will smash all our windows with a baseball bat. I fear this because it's how I currently feel about Rob's security methods. We pay the fireman twelve dollars to leave it there for three days and take a forty-five minute boat ride to our destination. A group of boys on the boat point to my husband and believe he is the actor Vin Diesel. This makes Rob very happy since he has been working out the last four months. It also makes Rob flex his triceps for the remainder of the boat ride.

During the bumpy journey, I look around as we pass small one-room huts precariously built over the water. Children hang over the ledge of the window and wave at me. I think about how difficult life must be here and how I walked away from a good job, a house, and security just so I could experience a different way of living. My decision seems selfishly out of place here. There can't be many opportunities for people in this area, and every day must bring new challenges. In the distance, I see a small wooden boat with a man rowing two uniformed children to school. People are the same no matter where you go; this father, like many others, wants his children to get an education, only he has to row a boat to get them to school.

The Bocas del Toro islands have a laid-back vibe similar to the Caribbean side of Costa Rica. With the wide variety of fish and miles of mangroves to explore, it is a unique place to hike and snorkel. Our boat drops us off at a hotel perched on stilts over the water: a rickety wooden structure coated with many layers of shiny varnish. A man shows us to our tiny shellacked room. The walls, floors, and ceiling are built out of this flammable lacquered wood. "Thank You For Not Smoking" takes on a whole new meaning here.

Our room has a balcony that overlooks a pigpen. I look closely and can see the pigs defecating into the bay. If my room catches fire, this will be the E. coli water I jump into. It turns out this is a poor island with inadequate sewage treatment and little infrastructure. However, the purpose of quitting my job was to see the world, and not just the homogenized view you get while staying at a resort, and watching pigs poop in the water where people fish is about as non-homogenized as you're going to get.

We spend the next two days snorkeling and body surfing, bouncing from one island to another. We visit Red Frog Beach, named for the little endangered red frogs that inhabit it. Many small children run up with banana leaves molded into funnels that each display a red frog sitting in the middle. Even at their young age, they know presentation is everything. In exchange for a quarter, they will let you take a picture with them. The children are smart and resourceful. They reward me with a big white smile and run with their frog to the next tourist they see.

On the last day, I hear about a recently discovered bat cave called Nivida Cavern, a place where you can see the rare albino nectar bat hovering over a subterranean lake. The more I think about it, the more I want to hike into this cavern and enjoy a swim in the subterranean lake. What better place to get over my drowning incident than swimming in a pitch-black bat cave?

"Do you really want to hike into a bat cave?" Rob asks.

"When will we ever get the opportunity again to see the rare albino bat?"

"Ten minutes ago, you didn't even know it existed, and now you want to take a dip in a subterranean lake. Brilliant."

Rob makes a good point, but I am feeling adventurous and remind Rob that we are probably safer in a cave than in our combustible accommodations. In addition, I am feeling invincible right now since I have survived a bullet ant bite and a near drowning.

As we are having this discussion on the deck of our hotel beside the defecating pigs, a young man named Kevin drives up on a boat and asks us if we want to take any dolphin or fishing tours.

"I want to see the bat cave," I impulsively say.

He looks surprised.

"Not many people know about that," he says, "but if you want to go, I know where it is. You have to hike through a jungle and then onto Indian land, but first we will have to stop by my house and pick up flashlights and galoshes. I'll go buy some batteries and come back in fifteen minutes."

He drives his boat away as Rob and I run upstairs to get changed. I put on a bikini and cover it with a pair of shorts and tank top. I slip on a pair of flip-flips and spray a generous supply of OFF on my body— all the while dreaming about the subterranean lake I'll be swan diving in. It seems a perfect way to end our Panama trip.

Kevin returns with the batteries, and we learn he lives in the jungle. The only way to get to his house is through a confusing canal of mangroves. We find a clearing, and Kevin disappears into the jungle. He returns with his wife, a bag of flashlights, galoshes, and a huge glass bong. It looks like the trip is going to be more exciting than I anticipated.

As we back out of the mangroves, Kevin and his wife take a few hits from the bong. The effects of the weed don't appear to cloud his navigation skills, as we are soon out in the open water heading to another island. We once again pass through a thick maze of mangroves before reaching an area filled with sugarcane. Kevin docks the boat and hands us the galoshes. After five minutes of hiking, I realize the boots are leaving large blisters on my ankles. I have no choice but to take them off and put my flip-flops back on.

I am hiking and enjoying the stillness of the jungle when Kevin grabs me from behind. "Don't step there. Do you see that mound? That's a scorpion's nest." I look down and see a hole in the ground surrounded by dirt. I carefully walk around it as Kevin's wife pulls down a coconut and cracks it open with a machete. (Apparently, she is having a jungle-sized case of the munchies.) She hands it to me, and I find a gooey substance inside; it tastes amazing. She explains there is a point in the growth cycle where the fruit inside has not hardened yet. If you catch it at the right time, it tastes like coconut custard pie. I finish my portion, and I've just started running to catch up with Rob when Kevin once again grabs me from behind.

"Wait...don't move... that's quicksand."

I look down and all I see is a patch of mud on the ground.

"What would have happened if I stepped in it?" I ask.

"Hmm... a couple of things. If it isn't too deep, you would only sink up to your knees. Then you would have to work your way out. But, if it was any deeper, you probably would have sunk up to your neck," Kevin lowers his voice. "That would have been bad, very, very bad."

I am beginning to think I've made a very, very big mistake coming here. I've even frazzled the pothead jungle family.

I calm myself and watch where I place every flip-flop step. Things are going better except for the aggressive mosquitoes biting me. They don't seem at all repelled by the generous blanket of OFF I sprayed all over my body. There are dozens of bite marks on my arms, legs, and feet. I go into a frantic swatting dance, spinning in circles as I smack the mosquitoes off me. I ask Jungle Wife if there is malaria in this jungle but she doesn't answer. Instead, she hands me a little bottle of oil to rub on my skin that she says will help keep away the bugs. As I rub it on, I notice the cloud of marijuana smoke surrounding her body keeps the mosquitoes from biting her. There has never been a better reason to smoke dope.

We get to a spot where there are two indigenous Indians sitting on the ground. We pay three dollars each, and one of the men leads the way to the bat cave. It is camouflaged behind a large tree with a river piercing through it. I put my galoshes back on as we form a line heading in. Our flashlights are lousy; they remind me of the ones I used on Halloween night when I was a kid. The beam is so dim, we have to aim all the flashlights at the same spot to get enough light. All four of us shine the light at the ceiling and see thousands of bats over our heads. They scatter, and I can feel their tiny wings in my hair while they brush past my ears.

I keep losing my balance as I swat the bats away from my head, subsequently falling into layers of bat shit. Didn't I recently read about the dangers of frolicking in bat caves? And how it was best to avoid rubbing bat excrement on my body? I've succeeded in ignoring that sound advice by lathering myself with a generous coating of guano. I try wiping it off, but the excrement just oozes down my arms. It appears whether it is bat or bull shit, I have the uncanny ability to land in both.

The farther I go into the cavern, the more the water fills my galoshes, making my feet too heavy to keep walking. At that point, Kevin tells me to stop splashing around and be quiet. He taps the water with a long stick.

"What are you looking for?" I ask.

"The last time I was here, I saw a crocodile in the water," Kevin says while flashing his light on the surface. "But don't worry, last time he swam right past me... uh... it really was no big deal. Do you want to keep going? The subterranean lake is only another hundred feet."

Before I can answer, Rob is already making an executive decision.

"No, we've seen enough. Just get us the hell out of here."

He didn't bother to ask me if I wanted to go any farther. All he had to do was shine a flashlight on me and see the bat turd covering my arms and legs. I love this guy; he knows when I have reached my personal best. We turn around and go back the way we came as fast as possible. We are almost out of the cave when Kevin tells us to look up. Right above us is the rare albino nectar bat. I couldn't believe it; it was as beautiful as I hoped it would be. We take a quick picture and continue our way out. I wasn't going to wait for the inconspicuous crocodile to catch up to me.

I braved a lot for this excursion: malaria, scorpions, quicksand, a crocodile, and various other worms and parasites I am sure will become apparent to me after the four to six week incubation period, not to mention a stoned tour guide with his equally stoned jungle wife.

"Unbelievable, you even wore flip-flops into the jungle. Next time, I'm choosing the activities," Rob says on the ride back to Costa Rica.

Maybe trekking into a bat cave to swim in a subterranean lake, with an equally subterranean crocodile, was a bad idea. But, if I hadn't jumped into that boat, I would never have met Kevin, eaten custard from a coconut, or flirted with my first pile of quicksand. And, I would have missed Rob's new obsession with renting every Vin Diesel movie ever produced.

What Would Fonzie Do?

The trip back from Panama went smoothly, and we were able to renew our visas. Overall, our mini vacation did not cost much. This is good, considering we will have to do it all again in ninety days. One expense that did surprise us was the cost of gasoline. Since it is about a dollar more here per gallon than it is in the States and is one of our biggest budget busters, Rob comes up with a plan to buy a scooter that we can use for our weekly errands. It will definitely be more fuel-efficient than lugging our car around everywhere we go.

"It'll be fun," he says. "You can ride on the back, and it'll cost us pennies in gas compared to the SUV."

"I don't know. Do you think it will be safe on these roads with all the potholes? People drive pretty crazy around here."

"No more crazy than Brooklyn."

"Okay, but only as long as I get to drive it sometimes. I'm not going to be the chick on the back."

"Well, I'm not sure that's a good idea. You're prone to being a little clumsy, and I can't imagine how you would handle a scooter."

"If I can't drive once in a while, then forget it."

Rob shrugs his shoulders and walks away. He's going to have to get used to the idea that occasionally he will be the one riding behind me.

On a trip to Bermuda a few years back, we rented a scooter since there was no other way to get around the island except for the bus. Rob emphatically refused to take the bus even though the stop was right in front of the hotel. Ever since Rob left Brooklyn, he's had an aversion to all forms of public transportation.

Twenty years ago, Rob and his buddy were going into Manhattan and got on the last subway car. They chose it because it was empty and they thought they wouldn't have to sit next to anyone. After the doors closed, they realized no one was in it because urine and feces saturated the seats and floor. As the subway drove along the tracks, the urine flowed back and forth like a mini wave pool, sloshing everything in its path. They had to hoist themselves, pull-up style, onto the metal poles overhead so the pee didn't splash their feet. This incident was the contributing factor to Rob's mass transit post-traumatic stress disorder, a condition that frequently has him lecturing people (with a fury one might hear at a Nuremberg rally) about the drug resistant strain of tuberculosis recently swabbed throughout the NYC public transportation system. If it were up to him, he would never take another bus or train again. I'm surprised he still does pull-ups.

With Rob not wanting to take the bus in Bermuda, we rented a scooter and toured the entire island on our own. Other couples at the resort thought it was crazy since we had to drive on the left side of the road. We even overheard wives telling their husbands there was no way they would let them rent one. Every morning, we drove off and could see a few men watching us, wishing they could get the green light from their wives and take off, too. We took that scooter everywhere, and one evening we crossed a bridge while the sun was setting over the water, an image forever imprinted in my mind. Although we could never afford to live in Bermuda, I definitely wanted something similar to that lifestyle. A scooter represents more to me than just a means of transportation.

We check out a few motorcycle shops in Grecia and find a new 125cc scooter for sale. It is one thousand dollars—similar to how much it would cost in the States. The owner lets us take one out for a spin without asking for identification. The only requirement is to return it by the end of the day. This is a trusting guy and not at all like the man we bought our car from. We take him up on his offer and drive up and down the mountain; it is as much fun as I remembered. We drive through town, finding it extremely easy to get around. Rob whizzes past traffic, in between cars, and around trucks blocking the road. Having a scooter would actually accomplish our errands faster since we wouldn't need to look for a parking space anymore. There is even a metal rack on the back where we could bungee cord our groceries. I'm sold.

The scooter has a current inspection so we pay and drive it off the lot. The first thing we do is stop at a store and buy two helmets. I wanted the cute pink one, but it was three times the price, so I decide on the reasonably priced black helmet three times the size. The helmet is huge, and apparently so is my head, not the cool Pinky Tuscadero look I was going for, but I console myself knowing I'll still get bugs in my teeth and wind in my face. Easy rider, here I come.

Once we're home, I tell Rob I want to practice driving. He tries to talk me out of it, but I am committed to driving this scooter.

"Okay, but first get on. I want to show you how the brakes and accelerator work," Rob demands.

I jump on the bike, but my feet dangle in the air.

"For heaven's sake, your feet can't touch the ground. This isn't safe for you or for me, if you can't steady the bike."

"I think I can do this. I know my feet aren't flat on the ground, but I think I can hold the bike up if I stand on my tippy-toes."

He shows me the instruments, tells me to start out slow, and walks away from the bike. I go ten feet before tipping over and falling into an azalea bush. Rob makes an executive decision (I'm subject to more of these recently) that I will never drive the scooter. I can't argue since I don't have a short leg to stand on. I have no choice but to be the chick on the back.

The next morning, we prepare to go into town and get some groceries. I hop on the bike and see Rob pull out a paper clip. He sticks it into the ignition where there once was a plastic switch.

"Why are you hot-wiring the bike?" I ask.

"Funny thing happened yesterday. Remember when I left to take a ride up that bumpy mountain road? A dog came at me and knocked me off the scooter. The little plastic doo-dad snapped off, and I couldn't find it anywhere, but no problem. I just have to start it with a paper clip from now on."

We've had the scooter for one day, and already Rob has lost the ignition switch.

We pull into a gas station and fill up the tank. It only costs six dollars and will probably last us all month. Spending six dollars a month in gas will surely offset the amount I thought we would have to spend. The longer I live here the more I find ways to live cheaper.

We continue down the road and stop at an ATM located next door to a sugar cane refinery. The plant has a treatment reservoir of industrial water situated adjacent to the road. Its long sprinklers rise up in the air like the fountains at the Bellagio hotel. At certain times of the day, the water shoots out of the sprinklers and splashes into the reservoir, across the road, and onto any vehicles that happen to pass by. It's fun to watch when we are driving in our car, but this time we are on the scooter.

I am talking to my husband right as we pass the plant, and I inadvertently get sprayed in the mouth with some nasty sugar cane backwater. Although it is a byproduct of sugar, it is anything but sweet. It is the opposite of sweet. It is fifty-one flavors of gross.

Convinced I am poisoned, I start wiping my tongue on the back of Rob's shirt. He tells me to start spitting. I try, but the wind snaps it up and splashes it back into my face. Riding a scooter is not turning out to be as much fun as I had imagined.

We get to the ATM. I jump off and glance at the reflecting window. With my humongous helmet and sunglasses, I resemble Rick Moranis from *Spaceballs*. I don't bother taking off my helmet and instead just let my gigantic head lead the way inside the cubicle. I stick my card in, and nothing happens. I wait until a message in Spanish pops up saying something like "Sorry... you're shit out of luck... no money for you." What? No money? Not something you want to hear when this is the main way to withdraw cash in Costa Rica. I jump back on the scooter and tell Rob that we are broke... destitute... indigent. It's only a matter of time before we, too, will be crapping in a subway car.

"What the hell are you talking about?" Rob asks.

"It wouldn't give me any money. How can that be? I'm afraid someone hacked into our account and stole it all."

"Why are you always jumping to conclusions? We'll just go to another bank and see if it will work there."

Rob doesn't get upset and is as cool as Fonzie. We drive to the main bank in town where two Arnold Schwarzenegger sized guards greet us, a common occurrence one might see in front of any Costa Rican bank. This must work since I've yet to hear any banks near me have been robbed. If I were a crook, the creepy armed Cyborgs pacing in front would definitely make me think twice.

We use their ATM machine but still can't withdraw money. We approach a teller and try to use our elementary Spanish to describe what is happening. She doesn't understand us, so we begin our Two Stooges charade act consisting of a lot of impromptu miming and hand gestures. Basically, we end up looking like a bunch of drunken street performers. She can't help us, mostly because she can't understand what the hell we want. We walk out with only five dollars to our name. We blow that on a bag of cat litter at the pet store next door, the perfect metaphor for the kind of day we are having.

Rob is about to drive home when I snap out of my anxiety-induced catatonia. Lord Dark Helmet would never quit. Wasn't I just stuck at the Panama border inhaling banana fungicide for two hours? Didn't I hike the rainforest in flip-flops with the goal of exploring a crocodile inhabited bat cave? I suddenly get a shot of adrenaline. I remember there is another bank not too far away and convince Rob to turn around. I don't usually go to this bank because I read that there were several cases of fraud where the bank stole money from its customer's accounts, but I am in a criminal mindset, and prepared to join forces with the shady underworld if I can get some cash out of my account. I jump off and run into the ATM cubicle outside. I rest my humongous helmet head on the side of the machine as I punch in my pin number, and wouldn't you know it, I get my money.

But, I don't stop there. I keep withdrawing money like I am on *The Price is Right,* just in case this is the last time I can access my account. The cash shoots through the slot, and I grab it with the manic enthusiasm one might see when someone's off their lithium. I keep stuffing the money into my Old Navy cargo pants, the ones my nieces said looked dorky because they had too many pockets.

I do a victorious strut to the scooter and tell Rob I got the cash, all the cash. I practically wiped out our entire bank account, and all our savings are now in my pants. Who would've thought our pants would see so much financial action?

Rob starts the bike with the paper clip as I watch one of the guards staring at us. It must look like we are hot-wiring the scooter and stealing it, but I don't care. I'm feeling like Dennis Hopper and tell Rob to gun it and speed away. However, the ten-pound bag of cat litter weighs down the back, so we can only putt-putt away. We leave the Cyborg in a miniscule trail of dust, not exactly the tough guy exit I wanted to make.

We are financially viable again. The thought of not having access to our money made me momentarily panic, but it all worked out, and as we drive back past the Bellagio, I keep my mouth firmly shut. I look around and realize it is not so bad on the back of the bike; I get to rest my enormous head on Rob and enjoy the scenery while still getting my fair share of bugs in my teeth. And that whole "Easy Rider" cool chick thing? I learned I do not need any more counterculture in my life. I think I get enough of that just going to the ATM.

Kooky Kayakers, Monkey Whisperer, & Pool Hopping

"*Nuevo vecinos*," Carlos says while handing us our water bill. He points to the house below where a new couple is unloading a truck. The Jehovah's Witness family has left, and now a Kansas couple is moving in, Harry and Carol. They are in their sixties, both retired, and are avid kayakers. They actually shipped two kayaks from the States and plan on taking excursions throughout the country. I immediately like their adventurous spirit. Who says when you retire you need to sit around and get osteoporotic? And why not do an activity that will have you in the close proximity of crocodiles? I'll be sure to give them directions to the bat cave with the subterranean lake.

This morning I see Harry walk up our driveway.

"Is Rob around?"

My husband walks outside, and Harry lowers his voice. I do a load of laundry, clean the bathroom, and still see them talking outside. Eventually, Rob walks in a little weary.

"What on earth were you talking about?"

"You don't want to know. Seriously."

"What's the problem?"

"You are never gonna believe this guy. This is what he says to me, 'Hey... um... you're from Brooklyn... um... Do you know anyone who will beat up my brother?' I guess his brother owes him some money, and Harry wants someone to break his legs. Why would he think I'm the one who could take care of that for him? Do I look like Sammy the Bull to you?"

Perhaps the motion sensors, the mace hanging around his neck, and the machete attached to his belt might have given Harry the wrong impression. It's funny that he thinks any of my husband's nutty friends from Brooklyn would ever blend in enough in Kansas to get this job done, like that accent won't stand out in the middle of a cornfield.

"So what did you tell him?"

"I told him *he* is going to get his legs broken if he involves himself with these kind of people. What does he think will happen? So a thug from Brooklyn is gonna shake down the guy for a hundred grand and just hand it over to Harry? More likely they keep the money, find out where Harry has the rest of it stashed, and take that, too."

I realize I need to come up with a plan on how to avoid Harry since my dog-walking route goes right past his house and down the mountain. There are no other roads, so now I'll have to take a short cut through the woods. Dolores is looking better and better next to this guy. At least she has never asked Rob to throw someone a beating.

Every day, Harry walks up the hill to say hello to Rob. Other than wanting his brother smacked around, I think he is lonely and tends to complain a lot about his wife. The move to Costa Rica has created a lot of friction between them. I'm afraid he is going to ask Rob if he can break her legs, too. After a few days of this, we decide we need a break from them and plan a small excursion to a popular town called Manuel Antonio. It will get us out of the house for a few days and away from Harry.

Manuel Antonio is one of the biggest tourist destinations in Costa Rica. It is a coastal town widely known for its national park and large monkey population. Most every tour stops there, and we are eager to see what the buzz is all about. Rob takes care of all the arrangements and searches for a good place to stay. He scours the Internet and finds a small condo for seventy dollars a night, but after pulling up in front, the condo turns out to be more like a one room apartment squashed next to a dozen similar buildings. Not surprisingly, it looks nothing like the picture on the website. We squeeze into the room, but before we have a chance to close the door, a neighbor is standing there welcoming us to the development.

"If you need anything, we will be right over there." She points five feet away to a balcony where her husband is watching television. He raises his hand up in the air and turns back around. "I love meeting new people, and you are just going to love Manuel Antonio." She leaves, and we begin to unpack our clothes and toiletries. A moment later, there is a knock on the door.

"Hi again, this is the time I usually feed the monkeys. Do you want to watch?"

"I thought you weren't supposed to do that. There were signs and billboards on the drive up saying it can give them diseases."

"Oh hogwash, take a look." She starts to whistle, but nothing happens. "Just be patient and they will come," she whispers.

I begin to hear a rustling sound, and out leap twenty crazed squirrel monkeys. I am amazed at the dexterity of their little hands breaking off pieces of the banana the lady is holding. I am also amazed that the woman allows herself to be covered with a species of monkey that rubs their tail and skin with their own urine.

"Go ahead, give them a banana."

She reaches out to hand me a piece of fruit, but before I have the chance to decline, little furry bodies smother me.

"Wow... okay... this is great... can you get them off me now?"

The monkeys climb up and down my body like it's a rope in gym class. She holds the banana up in the air, and they bounce off me and back onto her. Just when I think I'm in the clear, I hear a screeching noise above me. Out from the treetop drops a white-faced monkey onto the neighbor's roof. It paces back and forth glaring down at us. I can see there is a new sheriff in town.

"What does he want?" I ask Monkey Lady.

"He's not a nice guy. In fact, I'm getting the hell out of here." And just like Martin the incompetent realtor, she takes off.

The squirrel monkeys scatter and climb back into the canopy. The white-faced monkey jumps onto her balcony and starts ninja chopping things off the railing. He leaps up and down as his thundering voice echoes throughout the complex. Like a drug dealer, my neighbor cracks open her window and tosses out a banana. The animal grabs it, jumps back onto the roof, and takes off into the forest. Agitating a white-faced monkey was not how I wanted to start the day. No matter where I go, so do the crazy neighbors.

In an attempt to escape monkey village, we take a drive through the touristy town. Hotels flank the mountainous road; some are older, whereas others are luxurious resorts. I pull out my Frommer's and find out it costs over three hundred dollars a night to stay at some of them. "Gosh, they look nice," I mumble under my breath while my new musky perfume, Chanel N° Monkey Pee Pee, circulates through the air-conditioned car.

"I've got an idea. Why don't we have lunch there and ask if we can swim in their pool afterward?" Rob suggests while opening the windows. "What's the worst they can say? We are already wearing our bathing suits under our clothes."

"I don't know; I don't want to get into trouble."

"Come on. Just imagine it: infinity edge overlooking the Pacific… A swim-up bar… Finish it with jumping into a hot tub."

"When you put it that way, how can I say no? But you do all the talking. I'm getting nervous just thinking about it."

Rob pulls into the fanciest resort, one with large fountains in front of the lobby. He walks up to the front desk and starts negotiating at the reception area for a free trial of the pool and hot tub. I casually walk away, pretending to admire the furniture in the lobby since this conversation is too humiliating for me to bear.

"If we eat at your restaurant, can we use your pool and hot tub?" I hear Rob say. The next thing I can make out is, "How about I buy a couple drinks at the bar and I only use the hot tub?" I then listen as Rob speaks in a thick Brooklyn accent, "You got nuttin here, come on, the dining room is empty." After a few minutes, Rob walks over to me. "It's fine, we'll have a nice lunch and then hang out for a few hours at the pool."

"Are you sure this is okay?"

"Yeah. Come on."

Rob takes my hand as we walk into the dining area and grab a table with of view of the ocean. The prices are reasonable, so we each choose the seafood platter and two tall glasses of iced tea. As the salty breeze passes through, I quickly forget about the monkey lady and her legion of stinky primates. It's always easy to forget your worries in Costa Rica. We finish up with dessert, pay our bill, and head down a flight of stairs to the pool.

"Come over here," Rob says as he directs me to the far end of the pool.

I stand behind a large planter and place my pants and shirt on a lounge chair. After I get into the pool, I notice Rob grab my clothes and hide them under the chair.

"Are you sure this is okay?"

"It's fine; let's have some fun."

Rob dives in and joins me. I paddle my way out to the infinity edge, hang onto the wall, and peek out at the ocean view. I'm watching a sailboat in the distance when I hear Rob call me over to the shallow end. As I swim back, I see the waiter look down at us then disappear. I doggy paddle my way to the swim-up bar as another white-faced monkey harasses the bartender. He tries to shoo him away by snapping a towel, but the monkey runs past him, picks up a lid, and eats handfuls of maraschino cherries from a jar. The bartender cowers in the corner until the animal goes away. It appears the monkeys, and not the people, are running this town.

I continue swimming but notice the waiter keeps looking down at us. He brings over another person and they both point at me in the pool. Before I have a chance to ask what they want, Rob grabs me, lifts me out of the pool, and hands me my clothes.

"What are you doing? I want to stay a little while longer. We didn't even get a chance to try out the hot tub."

"Yeah... but we really should be going now."

He walks faster and drags me behind him. It has now occurred to me that Rob never got permission to swim in the pool, and we just went pool hopping... rogue style. We jump in the car and speed away, never looking back, our wet footprints the only evidence left.

"You know, you could have told me what you were doing," I mention as we drive toward the beach.

"Yeah, sure, like you were going to do that if they said no. And didn't you have fun?"

He's right. I probably wouldn't have tried it and would have missed out on swimming at a fancy resort. I would miss out on a lot of things if Rob didn't convince me.

Our next stop is Manuel Antonio National Park. We spot toucans and sloths as the monkeys jump around above us. One mischievous one leaps down and unzips a backpack someone left on a picnic table. The owner runs back, but it is too late. The monkey disappears with a set of keys into the tree. I can imagine the monkey pulling away in the poor sap's rental car.

There are secluded beaches within the park, so we decide to relax and catch some rays. After ten minutes of blissful solitude, I see two raccoons waddling toward us. It's unusual to see raccoons in the daytime, so I keep an eye on them as they march single file. They get closer and still don't show any indication of slowing down. We jump up, run into the water, and watch as the two ransack our bags. I'm getting beach jacked by two flipping raccoons and helplessly watch as

175

they dig into our sneakers, pulling out our socks and camera. They toss both to the side as they empty my purse of all its contents. Even the monkeys overhead stare down, too intimidated to get involved. Finally, they leave with a bag of crackers and disappear into the forest in search of more tourists to terrorize. It's not just the monkeys running this town, but the raccoons as well.

The next morning, we wake up extra early to avoid bumping into The Monkey Whisperer. We pack our car and begin the ride back. We recall all the things that occurred on the trip: smelly monkey assault, illegal pool hopping, and being shaken down by crafty raccoons. Once back in Grecia, I see Dolores walking her dogs.

"I'm glad you're home," she says while leaning into the driver's side window. "I have a bunch of bats in my attic and need someone to chase them out of there. What are you guys doing this afternoon?"

I'm almost happy to see her.

Stop... Or My Wife Will Shoot

There are bumps in the night and rumbling under my feet; earthquakes are common here since Costa Rica is located within the Ring of Fire, a twenty-five thousand mile arc stretching across Asia, North and South America. Most earthquakes occur within this ring, and I have already felt a bunch of them. Some are strong enough to rattle the house, while others make me feel as if I am trying to balance on one leg in a rowboat. I'm not used to this seismic activity, but it rarely results in any damage or loss of life. There are few skyscrapers and stringent engineering codes apply to all buildings. It will be challenging getting used to this, but compared to spending the day trying to get insurance companies to pay my outstanding bills, even living on a fault line, near a volcano, with potential mudslides is better than going back to work.

Aside from occasional shifting plates, I am adapting to my new surroundings except for the intermittent feelings of homesickness. I've found it's best to let these emotions unfold naturally and not try to stop or harness them. I've noticed the bureaucracy here can trigger an episode, each obstacle an assault on how I used to do things. Trying to get residency has really stressed me out. I've always been in control, but moving here has taught me that I must loosen up and not get strangled by things I can't navigate on my own. Rob assures me we will eventually get our residency papers submitted. *Eventualmente...* the most commonly used word in Costa Rica.

Today I'm going to visit Julie and Mark, our old Jehovah's Witnesses neighbors, and their five children. Since Harry and Carol moved next door, I feel it's even more necessary to remain friends with the few people who haven't peed on my lawn or inquired about my husband's assassination services. The Jehovah's Witnesses family, so far, has done neither.

Julie gave me a call and asked if Rob and I would like to have lunch at their new house. They moved across town near a small soccer field that, unbeknownst to them, serves as the location for one of the biggest yearly festivals. Coincidentally, the time I visit is when this fair is taking place. We park our car in the driveway, where four horses are tied to a tree. Fifty feet from them is a makeshift bullpen where a couple men take their chances riding the animals.

"Doesn't this bother you?" I ask, pointing to the growing turd pile at the end of their driveway.

"It can get noisy at night; they like to play a lot of Guns N' Roses, but other than that, it's only for two weeks, so we can live through it," Julie cheerfully says while waving to a man launching himself onto a bull. This family must have drunk the Kool-Aid. How on earth can they have so much patience? I am convinced they are on this planet to remind me constantly to stop acting like a buffoon whenever I come face to face with something that makes me uncomfortable. If they can live next to a bullring and a mountain of horse crap, I can stop having a meltdown every time I can't get money out of the ATM.

Julie and Mark have a way of accepting the moment and evaluating what long-term effects it will have on their life. If it is something they can manage, they don't bother getting upset. It's definitely another piece of the happiness puzzle I've discovered. The more I allow myself to go with the flow, the happier I am. It's not easy for me, but I am allowing myself to ease up and enjoy the moment. The "allowance" of relinquishing to a happier life is something I constantly struggle through. Perhaps giving myself permission to enjoy the moment is harder than actually doing it. However, I am trying and can slowly see some changes since moving here. Recognizing these qualities in happy people makes me reexamine past behaviors and acknowledge the things that have held me back.

Even with all the inconveniences I have faced, I can't argue about things being wonderfully fabulous here. There are many advantages to living near a forest preserve, and I don't take any of it for granted. I see more birds in a day than I ever did in a year back in the States. Recently, I caught a glimpse of a Blue Guan, two feet in length and bobbing his head up and down like a rooster. At six every morning, a flock of parrots squawk over my house, and I've seen a few green toucans digging in my compost pile. Just the other day, a squirrel cuckoo showed up and chased off a bigger Mot-Mot bird. My house looks like the backdrop of a Disney film at any given time.

The birds are spectacular here, but the insects continue to amaze me. One cricket makes a sound like someone trying to get your attention. *Psst... psst,* I hear at night while under my covers. There are metallic green ladybugs and devilish lightening bugs that pierce the air with two blinking beams of light. They startle me often into believing someone is staring at me through the window. It's easy to let your imagination run wild here, always envisioning strange people lurking around in the forest.

Although my location is a bird lover's dream, it also has a medley of little critters passing through. It's common to see a pack of coati (raccoon-like animals with long snouts and tails as long as their body) strut across my front lawn on their way into the forest. An innocent hike through my backyard will reveal deep, dark holes in the ground that hide sleeping animals. I often stand over them and wonder what lies deep inside but wisely know to back away and let the sleepy guys rest. Thanks to Dolores and her inquisitive dogs, I've also learned porcupines roam the woods shooting quills into their surprised doggy faces. As far as I know, Dolores has not been shot with any quills, but give her time—even porcupines run out of patience.

Having animals, insects, and my neighborhood calico cat constantly cavorting around our property makes monitoring our motion sensors a full-time job. The other night, our front terrace sensor went off at three in the morning. Rob looked out the window but saw nothing. Instead of going back to bed, he remained at the window to see if the interloper was coming back. After a few minutes, Rob saw what looked like a very large opossum playing hockey with the sensor (something that I would enjoy doing to the damn thing right about now). The rodent then casually dined on a ripe banana we left outside, and just to show us who's boss, he took a crap on the terrace before running into the forest. And just to show *him* who's boss, I stepped in it the next morning. It's disturbing that Rob did not share this information with his wife before she unwisely walked outside in bare feet to enjoy the morning view.

My neighbors from Kansas had lived on ten acres and learned to adjust to all the peculiar problems that came with residing so close to nature. Even Julie and Mark lived in a rural area before and were comfortable with the creatures popping up around their house. This is all new to us, a couple of clueless amateurs from the tri-state area. Short of going to a zoo (where I previously chronicled my first introduction to a crap-slinging monkey), I was never close to anything similar to the habitat I am residing in now. When the sun goes down and darkness blankets the mountaintop, I never know what animal will decide to visit. Tonight is one of those cruelly, quiet nights until Rob hears a tapping at the window.

"Did you hear that?" he asks.

"Sounds like a bat or maybe a bird trying to get into the attic," I say before we both go back to watching television.

"There it is again; it sounds like... like scratching."

Rob walks to the window and tries to see out. The darkness cloaks everything except the flickering lightening bugs. With a puzzled look on his face, Rob turns back around before the scratching starts again, more and more sounding like someone trying to rip the screen off. I quickly reach for our camera and snap a picture at the window. The flash lights up the room, and in that short moment, we witness a red-eyed animal clawing at our screen. It jumps down and darts to the other side of the house, jumping onto another window and latching onto the ledge. Not surprisingly, that sends me into an indefinite fit of psychosis. My following actions are no less dramatic than if Jeffrey Dahmer appeared at my doorstep holding a jar of barbecue sauce. I run throughout the house screaming while closing all the windows.

"Oh my God, it will get in. Close the windows… lock the doors. Where's the mace? WHERE'S THE GUN?"

I remain in a frantic state while Rob continues to take pictures. At this point, I am in full-throttle panic mode, not unlike my constitution during my near drowning episode. I am ten seconds from blindly blasting gunfire into our wall, windows, and maybe into Rob if he gets in the way. I have somehow transformed into Yosemite Sam.

"Come back; you have to see these pictures."

Rob shows me the camera, and after the first freaky red-eyed shot, further pictures reveal the creature was a small mammal, almost cute in its furry self. It has a long tail and adorable little hands that are holding onto the window ledge outside. Upon further investigation, I conclude he is not breaking in but is licking the insects off the window and screen.

"I can't believe I almost pumped ten rounds into him," I confess as Rob flips through the pictures.

The mammal eventually returns into the forest; its gait a cross between a monkey and cat. I take out our laminated animal chart and identify him as a kinkajou. Even the name sounds adorable. A kinkajou is a small animal also known as a honey bear, with an average weight of five pounds. It can be as long as two feet. Its agility often has people confusing it for a monkey, or in my paranoid mind, a serial killer. Since it is nocturnal, people rarely see one. We were lucky he jumped on our house. He is possibly the cutest animal ever to walk the planet.

His demeanor is calm, quiet, and playful: all of the things I've been looking for in a window-scratching friend. To think: I went running through the house screaming. It just goes to show I have not adapted to my rainforest lifestyle. Not only am I assimilating to a different culture, but also a completely different environment. At one time, I would have been concerned with squirrels in my attic. Not anymore. I have to start getting used to these things, like animals attaching themselves to my window to enjoy a dinner of tasty insects.

Today, I call Julie and Mark and tell them about my little guest. I leave out the part of me screaming through the house with a loaded gun, probably not something you share with someone you are trying to make friends with. They in turn tell me the fair next to their house played the entire catalog of Gun's and Roses as the festival wound down its last night.

"It really wasn't that bad, and I had a chance to listen to a bunch of songs I never heard before. You betcha it was fun." Julie cheerfully remarks.

I should have known it. If the mile-high turd pile didn't bother her, I doubt a little *Welcome to the Jungle* would.

.

Cell Phone Blues

My cell phone bill is seven dollars a month. I like to brag about it since my bill in the States was ten times that amount. It's the type of bill that would impress my dad. "Now that's a sensible expenditure," he would say. My father's frugality is legendary. My sister and I even hid our new Buster Brown school shoes from my father, knowing that this lavish purchase would spiral him into fears of bankruptcy. "A penny saved is a penny saved" as far as he was concerned, a philosophy he carries over when dealing with household repairs.

Two years ago, I visited my parents and found the bathtub leaking and the floor rotted. Rob and I both volunteered to gut and re-tile the bathroom for them. My father emphatically refused.

"This is not a job for you. There is no problem, so please don't get involved with my personal affairs," he indignantly replied.

Yesterday, I received a call from my father, telling me his bathtub was leaking and the floor rotted, so rotted, there is a distinct possibility my parents may be showering one moment only to find themselves crashing down one floor into the laundry room the next. They got a quote from a contractor for the repairs, thus the reason for the call.

"Nadine, the price... well... all I can say... it was damn near unconscionable."

I can only imagine the estimate for the remodel was something close to the cost of building a brand new baseball stadium, complete with a high definition JumboTron responsible for displaying every fart-nut proposing to his drunken girlfriend.

"I've put a lot of thought into this and feel that you and Rob are the perfect team for this project," my father decides as though I never approached him before with this suggestion. "I want you to redo the bathroom over Christmas break. At that time, I will take Mom on a Caribbean cruise, so we will not be in the house. Don't be concerned about food; mom will have plenty of egg salad sandwiches and ice cold RC Cola waiting for you in the fridge."

Just the way I want to celebrate the holiday—egg salad sandwiches with a demolition side of lead paint toxicity. Ahh... it brings back so many memories.

Stunted growth and delayed development were hallmarks of all kids growing up in the 1970's. On the one hand, everyone in those days ingested lead by just inhaling the microscopic dust that circulated in their suburban 1950 style homes. On the other hand, if you were one of the dumber kids like my classmate Billy Kaminski, you got your daily lead allowance by sucking on the paint chips while watching School House Rock, ironically making Billy dumber in the process.

My father's frugality is never far from my mind, and I wanted to share this seven-dollar cell phone bill with him. It would be a proud moment in the Hays household. But what I didn't want to tell him, and what really pokes a hole in my bargain of the century, is that the cell phone itself cost us three hundred dollars.

Three.

Hundred.

Dollars.

It's hard for me to admit that out loud. The problem is the

country is switching over cell phone frequencies. The Central American Free Trade Agreement just passed, so things are in the middle of changing. There is this new improved frequency, but we can't get a phone for it since there is a huge waiting list. We need a phone that will work with the old frequency, and unfortunately, it happens to cost close to a month's rent. What makes this purchase all the worse is that it looks like a refurbished Fisher Price phone my two-year-old niece might play with. Even Barbie and Ken sport better models than this.

Within a couple weeks of having the phone, all the "special" features stopped working, and what I mean by features is not internal GPS or forty different apps or even a camera. No, my features that stopped working were the only features this phone had: a calculator and an alarm clock. I feel like I have an Atari while everyone else is playing the Wii, and now my Atari is working like I spilled RC Cola all over it.

I occasionally see people walking around with iPhones. I believe they get their signal from Panama, but soon that should change when Costa Rica allows cellular companies to compete for contracts. It's just a matter of time before I'll be able to purchase an iPhone and have the ability to text, call, shoot pictures, and tell you my longitude and latitude coordinates. How did I get by all these years without Google Earth-ing myself? I'm the type of perfectly self-absorbed person who finds this feature irresistible.

The longer I think about how great my next phone will be, the more I consider why I even need a phone that performs all these functions. In the past, my cell phone provided a big distraction in my life. The constant calls and texts made it difficult to unwind. I was always multitasking, even while sitting on the couch watching television. I couldn't just let the call go to voice mail; I felt a strong urge to answer it no matter what I was doing. It was easy to fall into this compulsive behavior because everyone else was doing the same thing. It was rare for me to enjoy lunch with a friend without cell phones going off and text messages returned. Now that I've moved to

Costa Rica, I rarely go to dinner and hear phones ringing in a restaurant.

Having less distractions has also changed some of my daily behaviors. I don't multitask but concentrate on one thing at a time, whether it is cleaning the dishes or sweeping the floor. I don't constantly think about what other things I could be doing. Concentrating on the task and finding the quiet enjoyment of washing dishes or sweeping the floor makes it possible to have little Zen-like moments throughout the day. Training your mind to do less actually accomplishes more. I'm finding out that 'more' is just another four letter word.

Aside from my crappy cell phone, I am one of the lucky people who have a landline in their house. There are only a few spots in the box along the road for telephone lines, and many houses still don't have a connection. The best part of having a land line is the ability to get high speed DSL. There is no other way to get reliable Internet service. Through the Internet, I can use Skype to communicate with my family and friends without breaking the bank with phone bills. My father's frugality has taught me well.

The biggest problem we have so far with the land line phone is the high decibel crackly noise that needles my eardrum with every call. Sometimes, it's so bad you can't hear the other person on the line, and you end up with a bad case of tinnitus the rest of the day. This problem also causes issues with our Internet connection. We've called the phone company and Internet provider (one and the same), who come out to our house, have a cup of coffee, and essentially do nothing. In between pouring himself another cup of coffee and flipping the channel to Telemundo, the latest technician recommended we dig up the entire front yard and replace all the lines. Wow, seems like a lot of work just so I can email my sister about how big Kim Kardashian's butt is. But, with all my ideas about scaling back, I still can't imagine living without the Internet. God, I love the Internet... It had me at hello.

Rob takes it upon himself to walk out to the road and see how the lines are connected. He notices what looks like a bird nest but with further investigation realizes it's not a nest but a clump of corroded wires. There is no electrical tape covering the exposed ends, which explains why we have such a poor connection. I find it very strange that the phone company man couldn't troubleshoot this problem since Rob figured it out in all of five seconds. To cut the technician some slack, there was a very compelling soap opera on Telemundo at the time. Billy Kaminski should definitely apply for a job at this company.

"Get some black electrical tape and pliers out of the drawer in the kitchen. I'm going to be here for a while," Rob yells from the road.

I bring out the supplies and watch as he slowly untangles each wire. He finds the end, snips off the rusted part, and begins to twist and reconnect them. I lean against the pole and see two big cables with blue tape at the ends.

"What's that?" I ask while moving closer.

Rob drops the pliers and yanks me back two feet.

"What are you doing? Have you completely lost your mind? Those are high-voltage electrical wires."

Sure, of course I should have known that; the blue masking tape was a dead giveaway. Apparently, the idea of being zapped with 100,000 volts of electricity is best done at ground level where there is less distance to crash to the ground, and to think: my sister actually child proofed all the outlets in her house when she had babies. Here, the kids have to learn the hard way.

Rob spends the better part of the afternoon splicing, connecting, and taping the wires. There is so much rust I'm surprised they worked at all. Once he is back inside, I turn on the computer, and I get the best download speed since moving here. I might even be able to video chat with my sister without her picture freezing in the first minute of conversation.

There are things I am willing to live without, but it is clear I haven't given up all my vices. Having Internet service makes my life a lot easier. Every correspondence is over the Internet, including our ability to access our bank accounts. I could do that in town at an Internet café, but it would be a risk entering my bank passwords on a public computer. Therefore, for all my ideas of giving up distractions, I refuse to forfeit some of the technological comforts of home. I am still having a love affair with the Internet that I can't seem to shake.

The phone rings, and it is our attorney on our other line. It's hard to hear what he's saying over the crackling noise. I hang up, and Rob heads back outside to re-splice the wires. I am sure he will eventually fix the phone if the high-voltage wires don't zap him first.

Cheating Death and Finding Pizza

People often ask if I go off-roading in Costa Rica. I don't because the real challenge here is to stay on the road. It is common to come across a three-foot-deep pothole, identified only by a large stick with a white plastic bag attached to the top. We once saw a large steel drum in a hole that made me question what was worse: losing a tire in the pothole or crashing into the drum. My favorite is when the side of the road disappears down an embankment and a pole covered with bicycle reflectors marks the crumbled mess. All these appear to be acceptable warnings and require a keen eye to avoid, so what would be the point to drive off the road? It would ruin all the fun.

Rob and I decide to check out a new pizzeria that opened on the other mountain ridge. It's drizzling, so I urge Rob not to take the scooter; I don't want to be on the back in the middle of a downpour. We decide on our SUV, and since the pizzeria isn't that far away, it won't use too much gas.

Before going to the pizzeria, we stop at a small bodega that functions as the mountain's 7-11. It carries everything you need with the added ambiance of a horse tied to a post outside. I also like the resident drunk guy who loiters in front just like at my 7-11 in New Jersey. The drunk guy always yells some gibberish to my husband; I think he is asking us to buy him cigarettes or beer. It's hard to say, but drunk guy Spanish does sound remarkably similar to drunk guy English, a lot of slurring ending with a toothless grin. Rob just smiles at the guy and walks into the store.

I check out the candy rack and decide on a Snickers bar. The packaging is always outdated, and the wrapper usually advertises a contest that has since expired. This time it is one for the last Super Bowl. The entire wrapper is a picture of a big helmet, and there are instructions telling me to go to a website where I can enter to win tickets to the game. In addition to the old packaging, the first third of the candy bar is crushed. I always find them in this condition. I wonder if the company does that in an attempt to destroy the dated lot, but like the waterlogged Hurricane Katrina cars, and possibly the Cash for Clunker's rejects, they all find their way to Costa Rica. This lax quality control always gives my husband promising ideas for unique business opportunities in Central America.

We exit the store and leave the drunk guy to chat it up with the horse outside. We drive up the mountain for several minutes and find a sign for the pizzeria. It is hand written on a piece of plywood that directs us down a dirt road. We turn left and see the pizzeria fifty feet ahead. Unfortunately, it is in someone's home. I imagine that I will have to sit down in someone's kitchen while a woman in a housecoat sticks a frozen Tony's pizza into the oven. We decide to skip it, but instead of turning around, we continue down the dirt road alongside the mountain ridge. We don't have anything else to do so we agree to explore a little before going home.

The road is only wide enough for one vehicle. On the driver's side are coffee plants dropping at a steep angle down a three hundred foot canyon. The passenger side of our vehicle hugs the side of the mountain, which continues to climb up another hundred feet. We drive until thick weeds fill the road, and it becomes apparent few vehicles travel down this far. Rob looks for somewhere to turn around, but there is nowhere to go but straight. We eventually come to a fork, one way continuing along the ridge and the other taking us to the right, climbing up into the mountain. Rob stops the car to decide which road to take. I suggest we go to the right, up the mountain, and see if there is a place we can turn around. (Let me preface here that I usually give the wrong advice. In a way, I blame the following incident on my husband, who should know to never take driving advice from someone who just recently fell off a scooter into an azalea bush.)

We pause and assess the jam we got ourselves into. We have three choices: continue down the narrowing dirt road, back up all the way around the winding switchbacks, or take the road to the right up the mountain. Rob wisely wants to back up, but I convince him that the road to the right, the road "less traveled" up the mountain is our only logical option. We deliberate for a few minutes, but I plead my case with such authority that Rob begins to see it my way.

Rob sits silently in the driver's seat, puts the car into four-wheel drive, and turns the wheel while stepping on the accelerator, but after going a couple feet, the tires slip in the dirt and the car begins to flip over onto the driver's side. I try to scream, but nothing comes out.

"GET OUT OF THE CAR! GET OUT OF THE CAR!" Rob yells. I turn and lean on my door, but it is too heavy to push. I swing around, brace myself against the middle console, and push open the door with the force of my legs. I climb out onto the side rail and realize that we are balancing on two tires. I can't jump off because my weight is preventing the car from falling over. I watch Rob slowly climb into the passenger seat then out of the wobbling car. He makes it onto the side rail and stands next to me.

We both look out across the ravine and realize that if Rob hadn't stopped the car when he did, we would have flipped over and rolled down the mountain. Nevertheless, we now have another predicament; our weight is the only thing stopping the car from flipping over. Rob recalls that we have two winches and fifty feet of steel cable in the trunk. He is the only one who will be able to use them to get us out of this mess. On a side note, these are the same tools I nagged him to get out of the car three weeks earlier. I thought it didn't make sense to drive with them unless we were going on a long journey. I am grateful Rob knew better than to listen to a super-sized lack of judgment on my part.

Rob practices putting his foot on the ground a couple times and finally steps off. The car teeters slightly but remains steady. Like Batman, Rob immediately goes into problem-solving mode and walks around to the back of the car. He gingerly opens the trunk to get at the tools. As I hang on the car, I look across the mountain ridge and see people coming out of their homes to watch what is happening. We are inches away from a major catastrophe. I brainstorm how I can support my husband and help him save the day. As his trusted sidekick, I consider my options and decide to do what any trusted sidekick would do when faced with this situation—I proceed to vomit in my mouth. As I am about to hurl my partially digested and outdated Snickers bar, Rob pulls his head out of the trunk.

"Are you going to puke on the car?"

In that defining moment as I am about to let loose, I see how I must appear to my husband.

Since moving here, Rob has: carried me out of the rainforest after I was bit by a bullet ant, saved me from drowning in three feet of water, and most recently, picked me up out of the bathtub after a nasty spill (I slipped while reaching up to put a fan in the window. He found me naked, crying in the tub with a desktop fan oscillating across my face). Could it be that I am the weak link in our relationship? Wasn't I the Lewis to his Clark? The Bonnie to his Clyde?

Rob once told me that he is able to handle emergencies quicker than me because of his higher levels of testosterone. It gives him a burst of adrenaline that helps if he needs to save me or, in case the circumstance warrants it, punch someone in the face. He states I am lacking in the hormone based on his observations of how my hands flail to the side when I run and my compulsion to put cute hats on my dog. All this may be true. Maybe I am testosterone deprived or, as I'd rather believe, scrumptiously estrogen rich.

However, this hormone affliction is not going to help me now. I am not adding anything useful to the rescue operation at hand. Once again, I have become a major liability and my husband has taken on the unexpected responsibility of rescuing me from myself. Now, dangling over a precipice, Rob has to hold my hair while I puke? What a monumental disappointment. This is not how I want this story to end. I have to summon up the courage I know is hidden deep inside. So once again, I do what any trusted sidekick would do when presented with a mouth full of regurgitated candy—I swallow it and calmly tell my husband, "What? You're kidding me; just go back to what you are doing and get us the hell out of here."

Not that I need to elaborate on this, but swallowing my own throw-up is by no means the best way to quell the nausea that initiated me to puke in the first place. Cold beads of sweat form on my forehead, but I continue to hang off the car. Rob instructs me to jump off if I feel the car slipping, just to let go and allow the car to roll over. As I ponder the notion that we might lose our car to a three hundred foot abyss of coffee plants, I find that I just don't care. I am so happy we are alive that the thought of my car becoming a flattened piece of junk means nothing to me. It could roll down the mountain, end in a fiery Dukes of Hazzard explosion, and burn to pieces without one tear rolling down my face. I might even yell out "Hip Hip Hooray" and put on a party hat for good measure.

But Rob sees it differently. He believes he can get us off this ridge. He hikes up the mountain, testing every rotted tree stomp to decide where to tie the steel cable. He finds a strong stump thirty feet ahead, wraps the cable around it, and attaches it to the front of the car. He then ties the second cable onto the undercarriage of the driver's side, stretches it over the car, and ties that to a rotten stump. I interject and question whether this is the most effective way when Rob turns to me with gritted teeth.

"Please, don't say anything, not a word, and just let me get us out of here. Seriously Nadine. I'm not kidding around."

Rob has raised his voice to me only few times in all the years we have been together, but it is evident he will make up for lost time if I keep yapping it up.

I shut up for the next hour and watch him crank both winches until the car is steady and he yells for me to jump off. I leap to the ground and watch the car as it does a balancing act like an elephant doing a trick on a big rubber ball. It takes another thirty minutes cranking each winch, inch by inch, before Rob gets the car securely on all four tires. He instructs me to stay twenty feet behind the car just in case a cable snaps, consequently, decapitating my pretty little head off. With this as the alternative, you don't have to ask me twice.

In the middle of all this, two teenagers walk past us with a pizza. They barely glance our way, as if a car balancing off a mountain is a perfectly common occurrence. We eventually get our car securely on the road and drive backward along the winding road. Rob finds a small patch of dirt where he can turn around, and we are successfully driving back home.

Rob puts his hand on my leg and calmly says, "Wow, you don't see that every day."

One might think that driving off a cliff would not happen ten minutes from your house, but like everything in life, an adventure is always lurking around the corner. Because of this experience, I have learned a few important lessons worth sharing:

One: don't take the "road less taken". Even though it sounds poetic, the metaphor rarely delivers.

Two: never suggest removing tools from your car just because they make a lot of clanking noise when you drive. Men always have a good explanation for lugging them around.

Lastly: there is a good chance an outdated candy bar will make you puke. And I doubt it has anything to do with low testosterone levels.

The Parent Trap

My parents are coming, my mother surely packing her patented brand of soul crushing criticism. I am convinced if she were a superhero her snide remarks would be her super power. Most have immunity to her comments except her two daughters, born without any force field to deflect the laser beaming wisecracks such as:

"Why don't you wear more make-up?" or

"Did you wash your hair today?"

Even with my advanced education paired with my ability to run a successful business, I am a complete and total idiot in the eyes of my parents. And apparently a slob too.

"They can stay with me," Dolores chimes in after coming back from peeing behind a bush. "They should know first that I'm a night owl and a chain smoker, and they can't use too much hot water. They must like dogs, obviously."

Gee Dolores, do they get to eat at the table or from a bowl on the floor?

"No, that's very generous of you, but they really like their privacy, and I have to find a place for them where they feel comfortable. I've got a lot of anxiety over it because I want them to like it here and not think that my life is over because I quit my job."

"Well I can tell you right now they are going to hate it, and don't forget to tell them I was robbed seven times."

Dolores' dogs take one last sprinkle on my flip-flops, and the whole crew leaves to continue their daily urine blitz on other properties up the mountain. No, my parents cannot stay with Dolores.

What drives me nuts is that I have a guest room, but they refuse to stay with me. Even when I had our three thousand square foot house back in the States, big enough so they would have their own floor to themselves, they refused and booked a room at the Hampton Inn down the street. Evidently, nothing beats a free continental breakfast with unlimited jelly packets my father can stash in his pants.

"I like my privacy," my father reminded me as if I planned to hang out in the bathroom with him while he was shaving. "I hope you will honor my wishes."

As you may have gathered, my father takes his privacy very seriously. He is convinced that at any moment, someone will assume his name and buy expensive Broadway tickets. This is because someone assumed his name and bought expensive Broadway tickets fifteen years earlier. The shows were the standard musicals: tap dancing paired with spontaneous outbursts of singing.

Luckily, the police arrested the Broadway crime syndicate, and my father never had another incident, but ever since the infamous "jazz hands" calamity, he has been skittish about his personal information. Therefore, you can imagine my surprise when I see my father's name, suggesting him as a friend on Facebook. I click on the generic profile picture, and the only thing of personal interest listed is that this person loves Folgers coffee. A DNA swab of my father's cheek couldn't have provided better incriminating evidence. These are the email correspondences that followed:

Me: "Dad, did you open a Facebook account?"

Dad: "Why do you ask? I have never alerted you to this information."

Me: "Because there is someone with your name who likes Folgers coffee, and considering the last time I was home you were wearing a free Folgers T-shirt you got from filling out a survey, naturally I considered you the likely suspect."

Dad: "I am alarmed by the question. I did provide some information online so that I could get a free nine-ounce sample of Folgers coffee. I was then directed to a site called Facebook... Oh Christ... What ramifications does this have on my privacy? This is having far-reaching consequences I could never have predicted. Damn it, what do I do now? Are there going to be more Broadway tickets?"

Fortunately, my eleven-year-old niece was at my father's house and quickly logged onto his computer and deleted his account. The only damage from this diabolical breach of security is that the world knew for two hours my father was a fan of Folgers coffee. He never did get that free sample.

With my father's strict lodging requirements in mind and the predilection on shoving buffet items in his pockets, Rob and I set off today to find a place for them to stay. There are no hotels but only bed and breakfasts, an unacceptable option to my father. *A hostel for grown-ups,* he calls them. The only other thing we can think of is to find them a house they can rent for ten days.

We search Craigslist and find a place on the next mountain ridge about twenty minutes away. It is a three bedroom/three bathroom house with an incredible view. It sounds like the perfect place for my parents to relax and enjoy their first trip to Costa Rica. We locate the house, and two retired gringos from Florida greet us at the door. Darlene and Frankie graciously invite us into their home and offer us a drink on their terrace.

Darlene was a hair stylist, and Frankie an insurance salesman. They are both in their late 60's and decided to roll the dice during their retirement and build a home in Costa Rica. They didn't know any

Spanish but found a contractor who was able to build a beautiful house for around one hundred and twenty thousand dollars. What I like most about Darlene is how she walked around the work site with a clipboard. What she didn't tell the builder was that the paper was blank; she only wanted to look like she was checking things off and monitoring the work site. I like her immediately.

These are two people I can actually see myself befriending, and so far, neither of them have asked me to wrestle bats out of their attic. I admire what Darlene and Frankie did. I thought our move was risky, but if it didn't work out, we could always go back home and open another practice. I would never have considered it at their age. After a nice conversation about moving to Costa Rica, we tell them the dates my parents are visiting. Unfortunately, Darlene and Frankie's house will not be available then. Rob and I leave on a nice note making plans to return and have dinner one night. We jump on our scooter and check out another house down our mountain ridge.

This house is a three bedroom/three bathroom ranch on five acres in a gated community. We love everything about it except the only furniture in the house are two beds. Rob suggests we move our furniture into it for ten days while they are staying. It will be a lot of work, but it can be done if we have enough time. I walk back outside and see half a dozen hummingbirds flying back and forth between hanging nectar feeders. Swallows are diving across the lawn, snapping up bugs in the air. This is as close to paradise as you are going to get, and I can't imagine my parents being disappointed. It is the perfect place to convince them that I made the right decision on moving here.

The day before my parents are set to arrive, we pack our car with furniture and drive to the rental house. This time the gate is not open and no one is around. We peek into the guardhouse, but it is dark and empty. Absolutely no one is here except for a black and white cat sleeping under a palm tree. Rob and I have no choice but to park our car at the gate and carry all the furniture up a steep hill to the house. I go back and forth carrying kitchen chairs while Rob lugs up the heavy table. I have twenty-four hours to put the finishing touches on it and make the house perfect before picking my parents up from the airport.

The commotion at the San Jose Airport is not unlike the fight to get the last Elmo doll on Christmas Eve. You can't enter the terminal and must remain outside in the heat. Everyone ends up pushing for space in front of a large glass window. People lean over me, inevitably forcing my face into someone's armpit, as they hold up the names of the scheduled clients they need to pick up. It's this type of bedlam that I wanted my parents to avoid seeing. It is so crowded that I recommend to Rob that we stand across the street in the shade.

"Are you sure? What if we miss them?" Rob asks.

"How can we? We will still have a view of all the people coming out the doors."

This is exactly what I recall saying to Rob after realizing we didn't have a view of all the people coming out the doors. I frantically search for my parents and find them standing near a garbage dumpster in the parking garage. There couldn't be a worse way to welcome my tired parents on their first trip to Central America. They are beyond angry. My dad won't even look at me. They sit in silence as we drive back to the rental house while I desperately try to make small talk.

"Look out over there, that's Poas Volcano," I say as Rob swerves to avoid a cow in the road.

"Was that a cow?" my mother asks, trying to strain her head out the window.

"What? Don't be silly. Hey look out that way and you can see the mountain where I live."

The bumpy road is tossing my mother around like a pair of dice at a Vegas craps table. My father stoically sits in the passenger seat counting the free peanut packets he got from the flight. No one says a word as we ride up the mountain to the rental house. Thankfully, the gate is open and my parents don't have to hike up the hill. As I open the trunk, something remarkable happens... my parents smile. I couldn't have been more surprised if Elvis Presley walked out of the woods asking for a fried peanut butter sandwich.

The moment they step inside, all the stress evaporates. My parents are not used to living like this—high ceilings and a bathtub with a view of the mountains. My father walks back outside and watches the hummingbirds eat from the feeders. A white hawk swoops down onto a tree branch fifty feet away.

"What kind of bird is that?" he asks.

This is the first time he's seen a hawk. It's as if the bird was staged, part of nature's greeting party for my skeptical parents. "He's unbelievable, Nadine. And to see him so close, it's quite extraordinary."

These moments of beauty can even crack the hard exterior of my parents. I think they have finally let their guard down.

My mom walks up from behind and taps me on the shoulder. I turn around and see her hand me something.

"Why don't you put on some lipstick?" she says.

With stealth precision, her laser beam hits me square in my solar plexus. It's going to be a long ten days.

The Parent Trap: Part Dos

udiences watched as *National Lampoon's Vacation* took the Griswold family across the country on a road trip to Wally World. Hijinks ensue. Father swims with Christy Brinkley, and dead Aunt Edna gets strapped to the roof of the car. A family vacation always brings to mind the foibles that inevitably happen when you stuff four relatives in a car with a cooler of baloney sandwiches. However, I do not want to have any of these mishaps with my parents. I debate every tourist destination and comb through every travel book to search for the perfect place. With great deliberation, Rob and I decide to go somewhere we've already traveled, to eliminate the likelihood of getting lost. We are taking my parents to see the exploding volcano.

Ever since my ant biting fiasco, I've thought about going back to enjoy the area without being carried out of the rainforest by my limping husband. My parents won't be doing any hiking but can sit back, enjoy the active volcano, and with some luck, find nothing to complain about. Rob calls the hotel and reserves a private villa for the four of us. We will each have our own bedroom with private bath. As I said before, my father is not one to share a house, but this time he has no choice. The house will have a fully stocked kitchen so we can make all our own food and not have to schlep to a restaurant for our meals. Dad will have to take the chance that I won't rummage through his suitcase while he is reading a book in the living room.

There has been a considerable amount of rain, and the road up to the volcano is much worse than before. We drive around a sharp bend and half the road has crumbled down a cliff. The only thing alerting us is a stick in the ground with, no surprise, bicycle reflectors nailed to it. It is the universal Costa Rican road sign for *Holy Shit*; coincidentally, the same two words that come out of every driver's mouth when they come across one.

"Wow... is that the only warning they give motorists? Someone can drive right off the mountain if they're not paying close attention to the roads," my mother says just as we come across another bend with half the road missing.

This time, there are no reflectors or sticks, nothing to alert anyone about the collapsed road. We are literally only a few feet from driving off a cliff, a condition that provokes my father to vociferate the mother of all exclamatory, a blasphemy reserved for moments of acute excitability, often muttered by my dad after witnessing a neighbor's dog crap on our lawn.

From the backseat, my dad shouts, "What the fuck?"

"Don't worry; Rob is a good driver; he'll be careful."

I turn to my husband and can tell he is nervous about having my parents in the car. He wants them to have a good time and tries hard to avoid the likelihood of my entire family being medevaced out of a ravine.

While I was growing up, my parents weren't up for trips to fun places like national parks or county fairs. Aside from our jaunt to Disney World, we were a family of smarty-pants. Sundays were reserved for going to museums in Manhattan, a city my father worked in all week and abhorred, evident by the amount of cursing that transpired on the rides from our house to the end of the Lincoln Tunnel. The only thing that cheered him up was a free parking space. Nothing has ever made my father happier, not marrying my mother or the birth of his two daughters, than parking on the city street and not paying a dime. I was never as enthusiastic since in 1978 on the New York City streets, every piece of asphalt had a powerful stench of hobo urine. If you can take a leak there, you can take a leak anywhere.

We were also dragged to every location where significant historical events took place. These sites were not the kind of nose picking opportunities a sophisticated kid like me hoped for, like Disney World, the wailing wall of booger depository. Here, I had to look respectful and understanding, even solemn on some occasions. There is a picture of me wearing a Shaun Cassidy shirt standing in front of a Gettysburg monument, and from my expression, longing to pick a good one. Even my sister, light years ahead of me in refinement, briefly considered digging for gold to pass the time. To expect my parents to simply fancy a trip centered on the act of enjoying nature bordered on the impossible.

A short distance from the volcano is a touristy town named La Fortuna. Today is busy with many people walking in and out of souvenirs shops. An ATV tour makes its way through the street. We slow down as we watch a pack of coati loiter along the side of the road. Everything is going according to plan until we get behind a truck carrying a big palm tree that hangs six feet over its side.

"That doesn't look safe," my mom points out.

A second later, the fronds of the tree smack someone in the face as he innocently stands along the side of the road waiting for the bus. Only in Costa Rica do you get to witness someone sucker punched by a palm tree.

"Oh my, is he going to be okay?" my mom says as she turns around in her seat.

I watch in my side mirror as a few pedestrians lift the man to his feet. The truck never stopped, but to give him some credit, he most likely never knew he hit anyone.

In order to get to the hotel, we turn down a windy, bumpy road. I move my dad up to the passenger seat and instruct both my parents to hold onto the grab bar. No matter how slow we go, the car shuffles my mom around, causing her to moan and complain about her back. I find it rather irritating since last year they went off-roading in the sand dunes of Dubai. At my parents' house, a picture of my mother dune-bashing in an SUV hangs on the wall next to one of my dad dressed like Ali Baba riding a camel. I am all but certain my parents did not make a public declaration about their sciatic pain while cavorting in the desert. From the looks of things, their discomfort level increases exponentially with anything that is my idea.

The villa we rented turns out to be larger than expected. It has a wraparound balcony with an even closer view of the volcano than we had before. You can also see Arenal Lake, where people come to wind surf, kayak, and fish. The living area is large, and downstairs are two bedrooms with huge glass windows situated right in front of the bed. You can lie down and watch the volcanic activity while relaxing under the covers.

The sun sets while I prepare dinner, and my parents enjoy a glass of wine on the balcony. They are watching the windsurfers take in the last of the light, their images fading into sailing shadows across the lake. We can't see the crater of the volcano since it remains covered in a cloud, but there is always a chance it will clear up.

"I've never been anywhere in the world like this," my dad says as they watch two Pterodactyl looking birds soar over the top of the rainforest.

I believe my parents are starting to feel what most do when they first visit: an irresistible connection to a time millions of years ago. I certainly felt it on our first trip.

Rob and my father look over a few brochures on waterfall rappelling, canopy tours, and ATV adventures. It appears the only things my parents are fit to do are walk along the sky bridges or ride the sky tram. The tram is similar to a gondola but travels through the rainforest. It's perfect for someone who is older and can't swing from tree to tree in a harness.

Slowly, the cloud starts to shift and we see the glow of molten rocks shooting out the crater. At first, the proximity of the volcano naturally alarms my dad. "Is this safe?" he asks me.

I nod my head but know the reality is that one big eruption could end our nice family vacation for good. They retire to their bedroom and watch from their bed as the rocks tumble down the volcano.

"Ooh... wow... can you believe this? It's remarkable that we are so close and can see the boulders shoot out. I don't even need my binoculars," I hear my dad tell my mom. "The kids did good by bringing us here."

On our last day, my parents decide to rest, so Rob takes a hike by himself to a waterfall. Along the way, he runs into four women, all watching a small cat walking toward them. It is an ocelot, a smaller version of a jaguar. He squats down to snap a picture of the cat, but the movement causes the animal to run toward him and jump on his shoulders. He doesn't budge while the ladies take pictures with his camera. The cat sits down on Rob's back and starts to lick its paws and clean its fuzzy ears. All the while, Rob is frozen and afraid that the cat will begin clawing his back. After a few moments, the cat jumps off and bounces up a tree. It finds a branch over the group and starts to growl, looking down at the audience watching it. Everyone backs up and moves away, leaving the cat alone for the next traveler to find.

Rob asks a guide at the hotel about the ocelot and finds out it was orphaned, nursed back to health, and released into the wild when it was strong enough to survive on its own. The problem is, it still remembers that people equal food, and it gets annoyed once it sees you don't have something for it to snack on. It is creating a problem, and soon they will have to move it deeper into the rainforest. However, it always finds its way back and always corners those few tourists who just happen to go for a hike during its lunchtime.

Rob brings back the pictures of his feline adventure. We are all jealous, and if it were not for the digital camera, it would be hard to believe his story. It's the perfect example of the miraculous things you can encounter in Costa Rica. We pack our bags and begin the three-hour drive back. My parents appear calmer, finally realizing we are happy here. My mother didn't even complain as we drove the treacherous road back carefully avoiding the two parts that had crumbled away.

"As long as drivers pay attention, the conditions aren't too bad," she says as she looks down the foggy ravine.

This trip served its purpose. My parents are reconsidering the idea that I made a huge mistake in my life and have finally loosened up with me living here. The ride back to the airport is uneventful, and we all part in good spirits.

The trip was a success. I didn't ransack my father's belongings like he thought I would, and I made my mother happy by wearing lipstick for the duration of the trip. And unlike the Griswold vacation, no one was strapped to the hood of the car, but there's always next time.

Darlene and Frankie

It's hard making friends after college. The carefree experience of school made it easy to find like-minded people, especially if they had the same major and frequented the same bars. However, other pressures monopolized the years following college: mortgages, bosses, and family responsibilities that took precedence over making friends. Connecting with someone took too much time and energy. "You don't have time for people with time," my father always said. No statement was ever more accurate.

The many challenging encounters with the dog lady do nothing to change my theory on friend making. Dolores has a way of draining any hope you will find someone who enjoys your company—someone who just wants to have a cup of coffee without introducing you to her uninvited Indian poltergeists. Therefore, it is as much as a surprise to me that I have connected with Frankie and Darlene, the couple I met while searching for a rental house for my parents. I admire that they are retirees who enjoy dancing, entertaining, and creating the fullest life possible in Costa Rica. Instead of going into a retirement community, they both decided to pool their finances and build their dream home on top of a mountain ridge. It's a gutsy thing to do, especially since they are not married but shacking up. They make my husband and I look like prudes. Spending time with them convinces me that this move is worth the risk.

Darlene was a feisty hairdresser from New York and then opened a second salon in Fort Lauderdale. After a successful career, she retired and now enjoys cooking delicious Italian sausage and English muffins for her many friends. She even bakes her own bagels since you can't find any here; she refuses to live in a country where you can't have a warm, sesame bagel in the morning. But, what I like most are her many attempts at stashing every possible item she can in her luggage. Once, Frankie was traveling by himself, and Darlene packed his carry-on. While going through security, his bag set off an alarm and TSA whisked him away for interrogation. Darlene had packed a full set of professional chef knives in his luggage, even one for deboning a chicken. With that kind of determination, how can you not love this woman? Well, maybe Frankie might have moments of hesitation, especially after Miami Airport detained him for six hours.

Frankie, an insurance salesman from Brooklyn, is instantly compatible with Rob. They know all the same restaurants and can talk for hours about the best food in the city: strawberry cheesecake at the Vegas Diner, Chinese food in Bay Ridge, and the best Jewish deli on 86th street. Food is always the primary conversation when you get two people from New York in the same room.

Rob and Frankie talk as if they are old buddies from the neighborhood. They each have friends with wild nicknames: Jimmy the Claw, Tony No Nose, Piña Colada Pat, and Artie the Hammer. When I asked Frankie why Jimmy was called *The Claw*, he says he doesn't know. Rob gives the same answer when I ask him why Tony had no nose. I don't bother asking what Artie was doing with a hammer.

Frankie and Darlene bought a piece of land with an incredible view of the central plateau and started to build immediately. They were lucky they found an honest contractor who worked to keep costs under control. Nevertheless, they did share a story about a guy running out with their money for the kitchen cabinets. They openly share the ups and downs of their experience, information that is invaluable since many people refuse to tell you what problems occurred during their building process.

Listening to Frankie makes you appreciate that building standards are different here and monitoring the workers is essential. Sometimes they don't ground wires, and sometimes they take short cuts with plumbing. Frankie tells us the high altitude requires a water pressure adapter on the pipe coming into your house. I didn't even know something like that existed. The pressure from the mountain rivers can easily burst the pipes without this meter installed. They had to make sure the plumber included that with his pricing.

Tonight, Darlene invites us over for pasta fazool. She is a great cook and overwhelms us with a delicious mozzarella and tomato salad appetizer. She is a perfect example of someone who shows love to the people around her by cooking for them. The table on her terrace is set with beautiful indigo plates and matching linens. We eat under the many stars that crowd the sky like rush hour traffic. I notice they look extra bright tonight, or it could be that I finally take the time to appreciate them. Taking my time—the concept tastes almost as good as Darlene's cooking.

Darlene brings out dessert with more wine and strong coffee. To be around friends who share the same love of adventure creates a special bond. None of us wants to talk politics or complain about the economy, instead choosing to pass the time laughing and watching the dazzling city lights in the distance. A night like this always feels like a holiday, a night I might want to remember in a photograph; however, I don't need a snapshot to remind me of happy times anymore. I am living them.

A week later, it's my birthday, and we all decide to meet at a restaurant in town. I pick a favorite of mine that serves the best burgers and fish dishes. It's unusual to find good beef here because the cattle are extremely skinny; they are not the plump, hormone-infused animals you see at home. We take a table outside near a wall covered in climbing vines of honeysuckle and watch the hummingbirds dart back and forth. The vases on the table are simple coke bottles with blue flowers hand painted by an artist. It couldn't be more perfect.

After a few drinks, we notice a man walking toward our table. At first, I think he may want to sit with us. This wouldn't be unusual. Many expats are friendly and want to meet other people, especially if they just moved here. However, he ignores everyone at the table and stands over me.

"It may be the acoustics in here, but your laughing is too loud for me and my companions," he says in a thick British accent. "Please lower your voice so that I may enjoy my dinner."

I'm not sure what he means by the acoustics since we are outdoors and my voice has nowhere to go but up. He doesn't wait for a response but walks back to his table where three of the most depressed looking people are sitting.

"Well, he's got a lot of nerve," Darlene says. "What the hell does he want us to do, sit here with our thumbs up our asses?"

I laugh even more, and now my British friend throws down his fork and stares in my direction. I actually think his company wants to sit with us instead of him.

"Please waiter," my husband calls, "All this outdoor air and sky, the acoustics are terrible, could you do something about this?"

"Yeah, this one over here is laughing too much; she is too damn happy. Can you do something and make her shut up?" Frankie teases.

Then it hits me: I got reprimanded for laughing too loud. Me. Someone who not long ago was probably just like this British guy, getting annoyed by other people's happiness. Now look at me: sitting with new friends having so much fun that the sound of my laughter is annoying people. I've come a long way, baby, a long happy way.

After dinner, we stop by the theater to catch a showing of Avatar. It's an incredible experience to watch this movie in Costa Rica. A lot of the movie looks like my backyard, with the large floating fireflies and buzzing insects. It is as if the creators took pictures of Costa Rica and adapted them to make this animated world. The emphasis on trees and their deeply interactive root system is something that I can appreciate. It's no wonder most of us are depressed. We sit in front of a computer with a screensaver of a mountain, beach, or river. Our daily vista of the world becomes no bigger than seventeen inches. We stare at the screen all day but end up feeling like we are missing out on something. Maybe all that cement (the malls, mega-stores and office buildings) has made us as hard as the concrete itself.

The movie lets out after midnight, and the roads are deserted. We turn down one street and observe something large in our headlights. As we get closer, we see a horse casually walking down the middle of the street, his four horseshoes clapping against the asphalt. We slowly pass him as he continues undeterred down the road.

The longer I live here, the more I am changing. I'm opening up to people and finding something in me I thought was lost years ago. I'm enjoying myself and allowing walls to come down that I built up while working in my office. I'm learning it is still possible to have the life you always dreamed of, and there are still people out there who are waiting (and willing) to be your friend.

"You know what, I'm tired. Could you just call yourself an idiot?"

-Debra Barone (Everybody Loves Raymond)

It is three o'clock in the morning when I catch Rob tiptoeing into the bathroom. "What are you doing?" I ask while propping myself up on my elbows.

"Lie back down... I just... can't sleep," he mumbles before running out of the room. I sit up and find my cat and dog huddled together on the bed like two refugees holding onto a floating Michelin tire. I can swear I hear gushing water coming from the kitchen. I put on my bathrobe and walk out of the bedroom, subsequently, into four inches of water.

"What the hell's going on?" I yell.

I wade through the water and into the kitchen, where Rob is crammed under the sink wrestling with a broken water hose. He fights his way to the shut-off valve, and finally the water stops.

"What in the world? How did this happen?"

"The hose exploded," Rob says as he shows me the shattered mess.

I reach down and pick up a few of the broken pieces floating in the water. Just as Frankie said the other night, if you don't have a water pressure gauge, your pipes could explode, and ours just did; we have become a victim of our first plumbing catastrophe. Now we are faced with getting all this water out of the house, and there is no wet-vac in sight.

"But that's not our biggest problem."

Rob pulls out all our important documents he hid under the sink. Everything is soaked: immigration papers, passports, and the title to our beach property.

"Remember when you hid everything down there, and I said it was a bad place because it was right under the pipes?" I say through gritted teeth. "Do you recall what you said back?"

"No, but I have a feeling you're going to tell me."

"You said that there is a bigger risk of us getting robbed than the pipes exploding. In fact, I think those were your exact words."

I peel open my drenched passport and look at the inky stamps now blurred and illegible.

"At the time, I believed it. Now after these recent events, I can say that I was wrong, deeply, unquestionably wrong." He takes all the papers and piles them onto the counter. "I got up a couple minutes before you, went to the bathroom, and heard a strange noise coming from the kitchen. I walked into the hallway, and the moonlight was reflecting off a pool of water in our house. It was as if we had an indoor koi pond. I didn't want you to get worried, so I didn't wake you. I thought I could sneak in and clean it up myself."

"How were you going to clean it all up without me hearing you?"

"Didn't get that far. I just didn't want you to panic."

Once again, Rob makes it hard to get angry with him. Even though he put our papers in the worst spot in the house, he would have cleaned up the mess himself so as not to worry me. Either that or he didn't want to hear me repeatedly say, "You're an idiot," throughout the cleanup.

He begins placing all the wet papers, sheet by sheet, into the oven. The only chance we have of salvaging them is by roasting them until they are medium to well done. It occurs to me to take a picture of the great Pisani flood, but then I remember placing my digital camera under the sink too. I don't mention this part to Rob.

As I sweep gallons of water through the sliding glass doors, I think of all the other things wrong with this house. From the outside, it looks like a sturdy place, but if you look closely, they cheaped out on mostly everything. Rob had been up in the attic the week before and noticed the beams were too thin. He also saw a thick venting pipe lying across the width of the attic. Instead of using PVC elbow adapters to go around the beams, they jig-sawed holes through them to make room for the pipe. Not only did it damage the structural integrity of the house, it didn't even vent outside. This explains why the bathroom always has a gassy smell, and it has nothing to do with my husband's new cabbage diet. I have a vent going nowhere to blame instead.

I've already listed the electrical problems that have plagued us the minute we moved in: outlets not working, nothing grounded, and the occasional surge that blows up every appliance in the house. I had a coffee maker that dazzled us with a mini explosion one morning after plugging it in. Rob tried to salvage it, but there was no saving the device. It melted into a blobby plastic mess so I placed it on our backyard patio; an area quickly becoming an appliance graveyard. Rest in peace, Mr. Coffee. You will be missed.

It's as if this house was built to look nice but not to live in. Darlene was right when she walked around her home with a clipboard. One must be on top of the workers just in case they decide to jigsaw your attic beams. There is absolutely no way you can build here without being on site. You are in for a big surprise if you attempt it. The mini-explosion kind, water or electrical, pick your choice. Apparently, either can happen with this house.

I look down the hill and see Carlos and his son walk past the house with two machetes. My pajamas are soaking wet from sweeping water for five hours. Carlos smiles before seeing the river traveling out of my house and down the driveway.

"Problemo?"

"Si Carlos, mucho problemo. Agua, mucho agua."

"Ah. Agua... agua... BOOM," he makes a sweeping gesture with his arms, swinging his machete in a 360-degree circle. He points to the water meter at the front of the property and shakes his finger. It seems that even Carlos knows this house is built like shit.

I'm about to go back to work when I see from the corner of my eye Francisco smiling. He is actually laughing, granted *at* me, but he is laughing. It's the first time I've seen him show any emotion. I start laughing as well, since I am sure my disheveled appearance must be one hell of a site so early in the morning. They both continue up the mountain to start their day of weed-whacking. I feel good that I've provided some amusement for them. I'm sure most gringos do.

I'm actually impressed with Rob's ability to save most of our paperwork. However, what was once a stack of papers two inches tall is now two feet tall from expanding in the oven. Rob does his best to compress the papers into a few plastic bags. He assures me they will now be safe under the sink.

"That sounds pretty stupid," I reply, "but I'm too tired to argue."

Later in the day, I'm hanging up laundry when I hear a blast coming from the kitchen. I run in the room and see Rob holding his eye while gushing water shoots four feet from under the sink.

"Rob... Grab the papers... Hurry... What are you waiting for?"

"I can't see. I was checking the good hose, and it exploded in my face. I think I have a shard of metal in my eye."

"Well, shut off the water! All the papers are getting wet again," I reach under the sink, fight off the super soaker, and find the other shut- off valve.

"You're pretty unsympathetic considering I just got shot in the face with a water cannon," he says while turning the oven back on.

I should have learned my lesson and moved the papers myself. After Rob's gun in the fireplace inferno, I should never have trusted him with another hiding spot. At least no one is hurt; Rob's eye turns out to be fine. Maybe we'll hide things in the attic, right inside that useless vent pipe.

Dashing to Nicaragua

Homesickness, like a sudden cardiac arrest, hits me when I least expect it. It never happens during the more likely moments. Never when talking with my family on the phone or looking at old pictures. As I have mentioned previously, I tend to fall ill when confronted with some of the impossibilities of living in Costa Rica. The differences, which were once exotic and intriguing, become illogical and insurmountable. No rainbows and butterflies can lift me out of my self-induced funk. Strangely, my "funk" resembles a 12-year-old girl going through puberty: a lot of whining, huffing and puffing, and an occasional episode where I run to my bedroom and slam the door. My husband, after observing one of my outbursts, looks on like a father who can't figure out what happened to his once loving and even-tempered daughter. One of those funk-inducing episodes hit me today.

I have been working diligently on getting the proper paperwork for residency. We needed a bunch of documents authenticated by a number of government officials. I spent close to seven hundred dollars getting all the proper signatures and stamps. I have proven, without a shadow of a doubt, I am who I am. I gave the completed paperwork to our attorney, who confirmed it was all in order and said we would definitely be in the system in a week. We would not have to leave the country every ninety days. The next afternoon, we get a frantic call that he cannot submit our paperwork. Apparently, I am not who I am. The documents are worthless, and I will have to start all over again. Worse, our ninety days are up tomorrow.

If over the ninety day visa allowance, the police can arrest you for being illegally in the country. To avoid this scenario, and the embarrassment of finding out how many tamales my cellmate will trade me for, we need to get out of the country immediately to renew our visa. Never in my life did I think I would utter the words, "We need to bolt to Nicaragua." However, it's happening. As we did with our Panama trip, we first have to go to the National Registry in San Jose and get the necessary paperwork. Without it, we can't take the car legally out of the country. I am so annoyed by this I go to my room and slam the door. Nothing is easy here—except blowing seven hundred dollars and screwing up your residency.

After a good hour of professional sulking, Rob and I head out to the National Registry to get our car papers stamped. I tell the lady what I need for my car, but she writes on a piece of paper "no lights". I don't understand what she means. No lights? My car does have lights, and really, what is she, a mechanic? Does she need to inspect my car? I turn to Rob, and he tries to sort out what is happening. After a couple seconds, she points to the ceiling and we finally get it. There is no electricity. We didn't notice because many governmental offices and stores shut off their overhead lighting to save electricity. Even the malls shut down their escalators during non-peak hours. We are out of luck; she can't give us our papers. Rob tries to explain we need to leave the country immediately, but the woman just shrugs her shoulders. We decide to go somewhere for a couple hours and wait it out. Maybe the electricity will turn back on.

The only place in a five-mile radius that has a back-up generator is a store owned by Wal-Mart called Hipermas. It has all the similar departments, except Hipermas has a thirty foot aisle solely dedicated to Tang. I can't remember if I ever drank Tang, but I do recall a commercial in the 1970's showing astronauts enjoying it on their flight missions. It also has the distinction of being invented by the same guy who invented Pop Rocks. The product has oddly found a fanatic audience here in Costa Rica, a phenomenon only superseded by the incomprehensible love Germany has for David Hasselhoff.

After a couple hours of walking up and down the aisles, we decide to take a chance and head back to the National Registry. Luckily, the lights are on, and we go to the same lady behind the glass and submit our papers. It is not long until we hear the successful sound of stamping. Thud... thud... again and again. We are legal to exit the country with our car. I would usually wave my papers triumphantly in the air, but my dispirited disposition prevents me. I shove them into my purse instead and stomp back to the car.

We go home and lay out the suitcases for the trip. I grab my purse to make sure I have enough money for all the mishaps and roadblocks we may encounter along the way. I try to predict whether or not the border agents will need monetary "persuasion". As I lay the colones into neat little piles, I consider how far out of my comfort zone this is. Nevertheless, I have softened some to these interactions. I am afraid once back in New Jersey, if pulled over, I might just try to hand the New Jersey State Trooper a twenty.

Rob is alarmingly good in these situations. So good that if he, and not our attorney, was given the chance to submit our papers to immigration we would already have residency. I am sure they would even have validated his parking.

With our budget settled, we start out on our journey early in the morning. After forty-five minutes in the car, Rob asks if we are going north or south. He has absolutely no sense of direction.

"NORTH," I yell.

My abrasiveness and the fear of what else I'll find to complain about make Rob shut up as we drive up the Pan-American Highway.

It takes close to six hours, and many potholes, to reach the border. About three miles from its entrance we see a long traffic jam with eighteen-wheeler trucks parked in the road. Most of the drivers are sitting under their trailers having lunch. We stop behind them, unsure what else to do. A man sitting on the grass yells out to us to ignore the trucks and drive around them. Since we don't want to wait, we cross to the opposing traffic lane and into oncoming traffic. A bus comes straight at us before Rob swerves back, into a space between two trucks. We continue zigzagging this way, Frogger style, back and forth until we get to the border.

Before we have the chance to park the car, twenty people rush to our window soliciting their services to assist us across. The groups all wear white laminated tags around their necks that remind me of backstage passes. These laminated cards give the illusion they work for the border. I know they don't by what I learned the last time I was at the United States Embassy renewing my passport. A young American woman doing missionary work in Nicaragua gave one of these guys her passport after he stated he would get it stamped for her. He took off with it and left her stranded. While she was telling her story, I made a mental note to hold on tight to my passport if I was ever crossing the Nicaraguan border. Rob cautiously picks a small guy named Jorge who takes us through the confusion to the first line.

Every time I try to take our car over the border, I end up feeling like a drug smuggler with fifty pounds of heroin stashed under my seat. Even with the right paperwork, all nicely stamped with its pretty red and blue circles, it is still a difficult process. Today, it is even more challenging because the registration of the car is in my maiden name, whereas my married name is now on my new passport. Since the names do not match, the agent yells at me and tosses it back. Now I really begin to sweat like someone smuggling fifty pounds of heroin under my seat. I tell Jorge to explain it's my maiden name on my registration, but the car still belongs to me.

"TELL HIM! TELL HIM!" I yell.

When that doesn't help, my husband stands in front of me and simply hands the guy five dollars. The man smiles, stamps the document, and clears us to go on to the next step. We get our exit stamp out of Costa Rica, jump into the car with Jorge, and go over to the Nicaraguan side.

Like a celebrity approaching a long line at a trendy nightclub, we bypass it as Jorge gets us to the front for another ten dollars. I smugly glance at the other tourists waiting. Clearly, I am a third world diva.

Jorge and Rob step aside and decide what the payment for his services will be. Rob remembers what the fees for each step actually were. While Jorge was trying to snag a couple more bucks here and there, Rob was paying attention to the costs, and his small amount of Spanish was enough to know that Jorge wasn't telling us the truth. With that, he hands Jorge a well-received twenty dollars. We walk back to our vehicle, where I find the ten-year-old boy who was supposed to be watching our car sleeping under a tree. I wake him and hand him one dollar. He gives me a big smile and walks off barefoot down the dirty road. I hope he finds another car to watch near another tree to nap under.

Once over the border, I finally relax. I forget about being homesick as the road passes Lake Nicaragua, the largest lake in Central America and the twenty-first largest lake in the world. It is home to the bull shark, capable of jumping rapids like a salmon to make its way into a freshwater environment. In the middle of the lake is Ometepe Island, formed by two volcanoes. This is not how I pictured Nicaragua. The road is newly paved (a rare luxury in Costa Rica), and there is nothing here that would remind you of their bloody civil war. There are even wind turbines catching the breeze along the lake and generating clean energy. We continue down the road and pass children in blue and white uniforms jumping rope in a grassless schoolyard. The school buildings are small structures with two outhouses in the back. The inside of our car is hot even with the air conditioning blasting. I can only imagine the sweltering conditions for the children while they are trying to study.

Before we left for this trip, I read about a popular area only thirty minutes from the border. San Juan del Sur is a quiet beach town and a favorite destination for surfers. If one is doubtful where to go, it is always a good idea to follow a surfers route. They are never pretentious, and their only agenda is to find the perfect wave; coincidently, the perfect waves are usually in the more beautiful locations. We stop at a resort that advertises specifically to gringos coming from Costa Rica to renew their visa. It has a three-day package for three hundred dollars. This is pricey since surfers usually stay at hostels for fifteen dollars a day, but I am not a surfer, and although I like to convince myself that I rough it on these trips, I don't want to stay in a place where I share my bathroom with ten guys. Therefore, we splurge and check into the Palmero Resort.

The resort is actually fifty individual two-story villas. They all have ocean views and center around a common pool and restaurant. Rob knows that we shouldn't even bother looking anywhere else. We will end up here because I have a habit of always going back to the nicest place. Once checking, in we observe that we are the only guests. The dismal economy is crushing Nicaragua. That, and the uncertainty President Ortega brings to the country. Like his Venezuelan buddy Chavez, Ortega, too is trying to change the constitution so that he can stay in power indefinitely. This has brought the country to a crushing economic halt, but the hotel manager is all smiles and has towering optimism for the future.

"Things are slow here, but we want the blond hair people to come back," he says. "Please tell the Americans to come and visit our country again."

He hands us the keys and gives directions to our villa. The villa has two bedrooms, two bathrooms, and a fully stocked kitchen. The living room is equipped with cable television, surround sound, and a DVD player. I don't know where else I could get these kinds of amenities for the price we are paying. I don't know why I ever complained about coming here.

We drive five minutes to the beach and look for a place to have lunch. Adjacent to the sand is a big selection of restaurants that face the ocean. We pick one with an elegantly thatched roof rising forty feet in the air and a dining area with expansive views of the ocean. We pick a table that overlooks a group of children playing baseball in the sand. The customers are barefoot, and we follow the trend, taking off our shoes and letting the warm ocean air sweep over our toes. There is a group of teenagers playing in the water, and we see police officers walking the beach. Many Nicaraguan vendors selling pottery, jewelry, and sunglasses approach us. It is interesting to see so many Nicaraguans with blue eyes. The color captures the deep blues of the sea and contrasts beautifully against their skin. Rob buys a pair of "authentic" Oakley's for five dollars. After that vendor leaves, a girl with her younger brother approaches me with a big basket on her head. She brings it down to show me individual bags of peanuts. I don't take any peanuts but give her a dollar anyway.

Our waiter walks up quickly, and Rob orders a plate of lobster tails smothered in butter and garlic for ten dollars while I choose pasta with clams for the same price. Both dishes come with garlic bread and sides of rice with shrimp. The waiter fusses over us, taking away our empty dishes and wiping away the crumbs. He moves the water glass to one side, then back over, only to move it once again. His inexperience along with his desire to please makes this lunch all the more memorable. The entire bill, including drinks and tip, comes to twenty-five dollars. It is a wonderful experience and you couldn't have asked for a prettier view.

While sitting back in my chair and enjoying the last sip of my Nicaraguan beer, I look out at the cliffs overlooking the crescent-shaped bay. Perched high on top is the second largest Jesus statue in the world, behind Christ the Redeemer in Rio. He stands with one arm stretched out blessing the fisherman in the harbor. It is the best way to begin our first day in Nicaragua.

Before we go back to the resort, I stop at an Internet cafe to email my family. It is a small, dark room with no air conditioning. Rob decides to wait outside while I contact my family and let them know I made it here safe. A minute later, an older, drunk American man stumbles to a station and tries to get online. He is obviously too inebriated to focus and starts to yell for someone to help him. Within a split second, Rob is standing over me, creating a barrier between me and the boisterous man. With his arms crossed and his newly acquired Oakley knock-offs, he looks like Arnold Schwarzenegger from *The Terminator*. In many ways, Rob watches over me like the Jesus statue watches over the fishermen.

Overall, the trip surpasses all my expectations. We have a great time taking an hour-long ferry ride to Ometepe Island, only to find out many of the ferries capsize and promptly take the same ferry back. At the resort, we float for hours in the pool, and since we are the only ones there, it feels like our own private estate.

Although we encounter some of the same problems at the border on the ride back, I have an entirely different attitude. There will be no more adolescent outbursts and foolish eruptions of hot air. My homesickness taught me what fear can do, how it can glue you in one place and prevent you from identifying all the fabulous possibilities that present themselves. I should have viewed my visa renewal as the perfect opportunity to visit Nicaragua. I will be ready next time.

Confronting homesickness is challenging, but if you do it without fearing the future, you might unleash a glorious new adventure you would never have planned on otherwise. And who knows: you may find yourself at a dusty border bribing immigration officials, to ultimately rest where Jesus greets the sea.

Happier Than A Billionaire

It's been fifty-two Fridays since I used the remote to open the hydraulic gate. Within that time, Carlos has given me a dozen excuses why he is waiting. Whether it's a missing part, bad weather, or his busy weed-wacking schedule, the gate has remained in a suspended state of disrepair, and after today, I am sure it will never be fixed.

Rob took the cat to the vet this morning, and instead of getting out of the car and unlocking the King Kong lock, he drove his car through the damn thing. I go to the scene of the crime and see metal shards scattered on the ground.

"I didn't blast through it," he says as I pick up all incriminating evidence. "I thought the lock was off, so all I did was tap the gate with my car and I ended up breaking it. It was too late when I noticed the lock was on the other side. Believe me, it was an accident."

"How can you call driving through a wrought iron gate an accident?"

"What do you think: I planned to break it?"

Carlos walks toward us with a ladder and looks at the broken piece of gate in my hand. Now it looks like I did it. Carlos doesn't seem bothered by it at all and says he'll fix it by next Friday. I'm thankful he didn't yell at me. But why would he? Carlos has been nothing but kind to us since the day we moved in. He has suffered through our awful Spanish, warned us about getting blown up at Arenal Volcano, and advised us about the dangers of San Jose. He has shown me more kindness than I ever did to someone in my own country who didn't speak my language. It's a harsh lesson when you can reflect on your own smugness and someone else's patience.

Carlos takes his ladder and leans it against a plantain tree. He skillfully climbs it and hacks off a huge bunch of plantains. He slings it over his shoulder and carries the ladder back down the mountain. I wonder how much they pay him for maintaining this development. Perhaps it's not much, and these plantains are necessary to help feed his family. No wonder he doesn't care about fixing the gate. I wouldn't, either. He must also wonder why it's such a big deal: all you have to do is get out of the car to unlock it, but gringos are not like Ticos. We have drive-thrus for everything: dry cleaners, coffee shops, liquor stores, and fast food chains that, ironically, should be making us get out of our car and walk a little before consuming our three thousand calorie lunch. America is now becoming a drive-thru life. Perhaps we all need to get out of the car once in a while, if not to open a gate, then to remember that your environment is more beautiful when not surrounded by a dashboard and cup holders.

Speaking of fast food restaurants, we rarely go to one anymore. There are few here, and they seem outrageously priced when compared to a fifty cent pineapple. Rob has already lost forty pounds, and my extra saddlebag weight has melted away. It feels great knowing I am finally eating a healthy diet rich in the vitamins and minerals my body needs. My head doesn't feel cloudy anymore and is clear and focused. All we did was follow what the Ticos eat: a menu that coincides perfectly with our new budget. There are no pricey meal plans or processed frozen foods, only fresh produce every day. It was obvious what we needed to do, but it seemed so hard eating this way while we were working. Taking a break gave me the ability to regroup and clean up my diet. I'm not only happier than a billionaire, but healthier as well. I want these new habits to be part of my daily routine, no matter if I go back to work or not.

Today, my attorney calls and tells me our residency papers went through. We do not have to leave the country every ninety days, and we can sign up for cheap health insurance that covers us one hundred percent. Next time I run to the Nicaraguan border, it will be for fun and not to renew a visa. Everything did work out, just like my husband said it would. I usually hate it when he is right; however, this time I am ecstatic.

I haven't seen Dolores yet today, but I'm sure she will show up soon. I roll up my yoga mat and bring in Rob's free weights. A little preparation goes a long way when it comes to her visits. She'll not only bring her dogs but her many grievances on how bad her life is. She complains so much about living here that she has lost the ability to see any of the positives, like the obvious one: she gets to walk her five dogs through a forest reserve every day.

Dolores' world is full of what is wrong in her life. Maybe I am friends with her because she is a mirror of me. I was Dolores: irritable and insolent most of the days at my office. I, too was blind to all the positive things happening around me. It was as if I was stuck inside a lousy video game, frozen on the same screen, and never being able to jump to the next level. This is where Dolores finds herself: stuck on one screen of her life, unable to get past the seven robberies and her kleptomaniac poltergeists. Maybe she is in my life to remind me what can happen when you lose perspective and only concentrate on the negative.

As cantankerous as Dolores is, Frankie and Darlene are the opposite. They are fun to be around and always have me laughing at their interesting relationship. Frankie is visiting the States for a couple weeks and has been instructed by Darlene to bring back a variety of unconventional items: a chilled cooler of prosciutto, a jar of Molasses, a five-pound bag of decaffeinated coffee, a stainless steel food processor, and a set of dishes. My bet is that Frankie doesn't bring anything back and Darlene is on her own. After his last airport mishap, poor Frankie is probably on a watch list, airport security forever scrutinizing the sixty-nine-year-old man who once tried to bring ten butcher knives onto a plane.

Our new Kansas neighbors moved out; no one seems to last in Jim's house. They told us it was too chilly in the mountains, but I believe they felt too isolated. Jim should be back from the Caribbean soon, perhaps with a new name as well. Once again, there is no furniture in the house. Once again, I know this by peeking in the windows.

A Costa Rican couple broke ground on the lot next door to Jim's house. I watch from my window as they go over plans with their contractor. I also notice they bring their six dogs with them.

The thought of this makes me consider if I should move. I can handle five dogs, but eleven might send me over the edge. However, it doesn't bother me too much now. The best thing I've learned since living here is to keep a cool head. By staying calm, I can analyze what is making me angry, and most of the time it really isn't a big deal. Since moving here, I've been able to get rid of that awful temper, the same temper that kept me from appreciating the lovely Rachel Ray.

I was so jealous of her perky personality, I didn't bother to notice that her show is quite enjoyable. She provides easy, affordable recipes for families and has an entire line of her own cooking products. I should have admired this businesswoman instead of despising her. All that smiling she does might be because she really believes in what she is doing. Her show now reminds me to believe in myself again.

We can all reinvent ourselves if we filter through the many distractions and concentrate on the important things in life. I would like to think Costa Rica possesses some kind of magic that helped me through my own difficulties, that my transformation is solely due to this place and would never have occurred if I hadn't picked this specific country. However, I don't believe that is true. The most important thing was my ability to recognize a metamorphosis was past due. Hitting the pause button was just what I needed. It gave me a chance to take a breath and reclaim the gratitude I lost along the way. When I finally allowed that to happen the gifts came in many forms: new friends welcoming me into their lives, kind strangers helping me learn Spanish, and the blessing of residing near a fearless, screen-scratching kinkajou.

By living a zero hour workweek, I was able to shed the excess and find my authentic self again. The big house and fancy clothes didn't cultivate the happiness I desperately sought because they weren't what I actually needed. There is a quote by the Chinese monk Wu-men, "If your mind isn't clouded by unnecessary things, it is the best season of your life." It does feel like my best season, and I hope I don't screw it up.

I gather the wet laundry and walk outside to the clothesline. Rob follows me and grabs a few clothespins. "You know, we've been here for a year and will soon get our residency cards. Why don't we move to the beach and start building on our property? I know our finances are tight, but I've been looking into cheaper alternatives to the classic concrete house. There are a lot of things out there. What do you think of shipping containers?"

"The steel ones you see at sea ports?"

"Yup, those exact ones."

"I'm thinking I don't want to live in one," I say as Rob helps me hang laundry. This is peculiar because he never helps me hang laundry.

"Okay, then I guess I won't ask your opinion on waterless composting toilets."

I abandon him alongside the pile of wet clothes and walk back into the house. Knowing my husband, I have another adventure waiting for me.

"Hey... come back. Honey... seriously... How bad can it be?"

You're exactly right, Rob... How bad can it be.

ABOUT THE AUTHOR

When not writing, Nadine enjoys traveling and convincing her husband that her homemade bean burgers taste just as good as beef. You can find her at the beach, riding on the back of a scooter, or frantically tossing scorpions out of her bed.

She shows up weekly at her blog to share these adventures.

www.happierthanabillionaire.com
www.facebook.com/happierthanabillionaire.com

CPSIA information can be obtained
at www.ICGtesting.com
Printed in the USA
LVOW04s1613170216

475540LV00011B/168/P